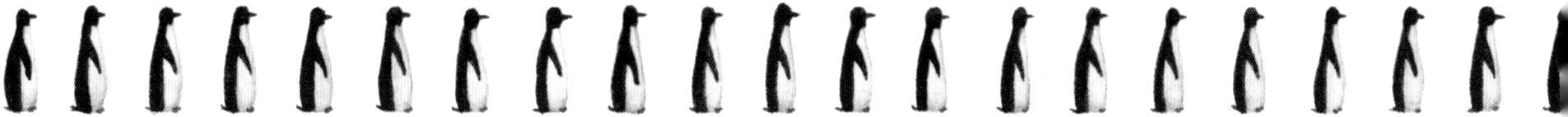

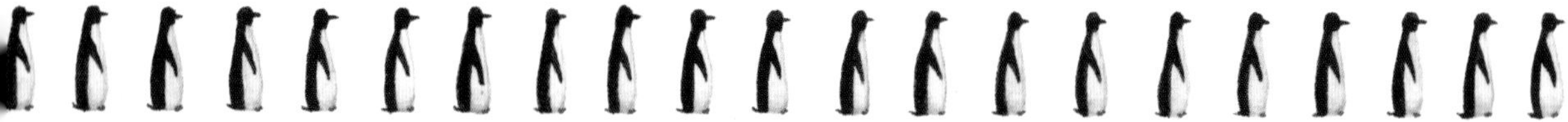

PENGUINS HATE STUFF

GREG STONES

CHRONICLE BOOKS

SAN FRANCISCO

Library of Congress Cataloging-in-Publication Data

Stones, Greg.
  Penguins hate stuff / Greg Stones.
      pages cm
  ISBN 978-1-4521-2550-3
1. Penguins--Humor. I. Title.

  PN6231.P34S86 2013
  818'.602--dc23

                    2013001828.

Manufactured in China
Designed by Michael Morris

10 9 8 7 6 5 4

Chronicle Books LLC
680 Second Street
San Francisco, California 94107
www.chroniclebooks.com

Chronicle Books publishes distinctive books and gifts. From
award-winning children's titles, best-selling cookbooks, and
eclectic pop culture to acclaimed works of art and design,
stationery, andjournals, we craft publishing that's instantly
recognizable for its spirit and creativity. Enjoy our publishing
and become part of our community at www.chroniclebooks.com.

FSC
MIX
Paper
FSC® C008047

PENGUINS
HATE . . .

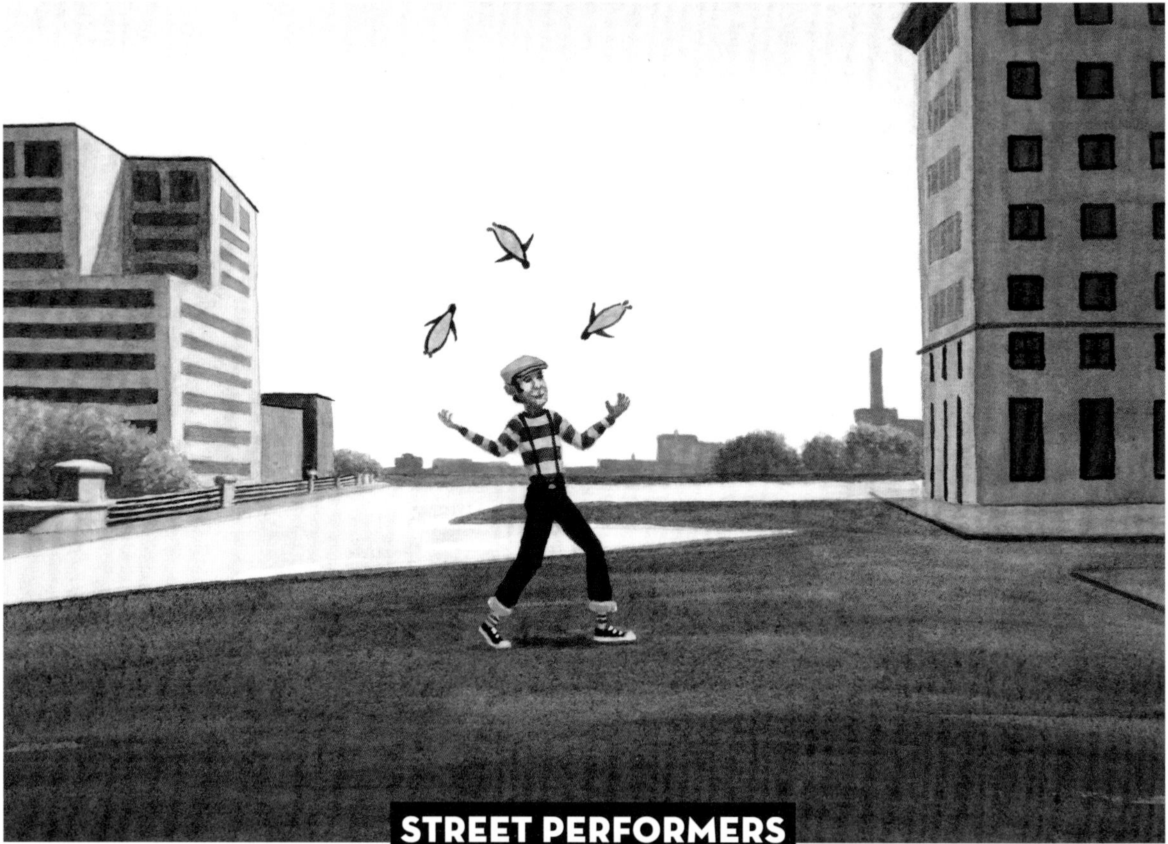

STREET PERFORMERS

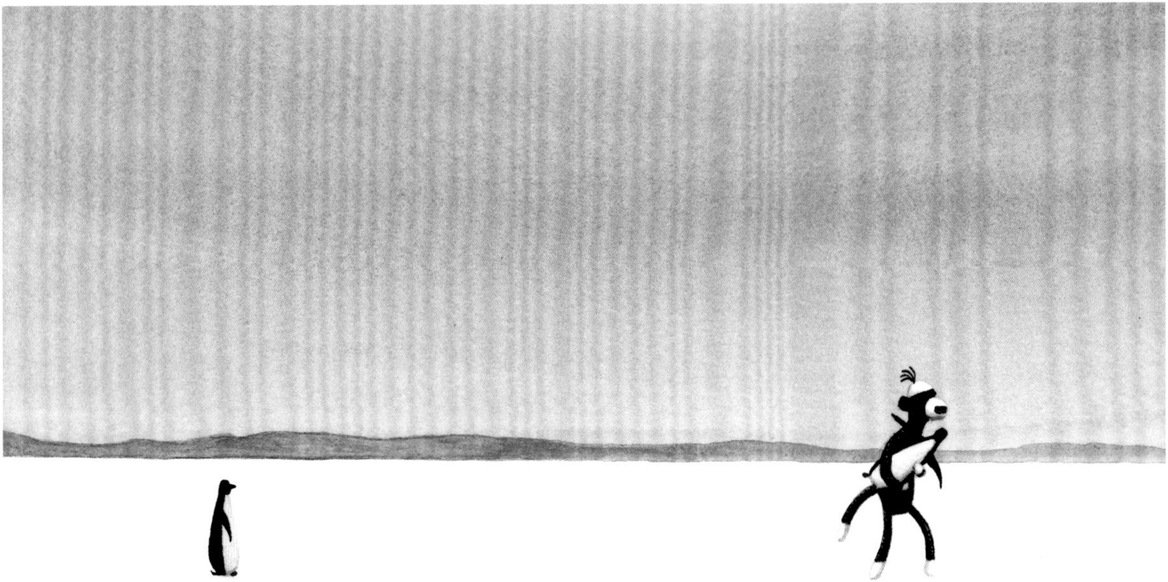

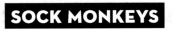

SOCK MONKEYS

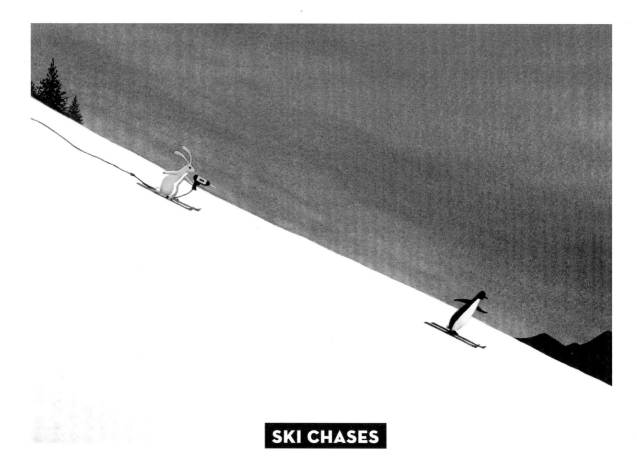

SKI CHASES

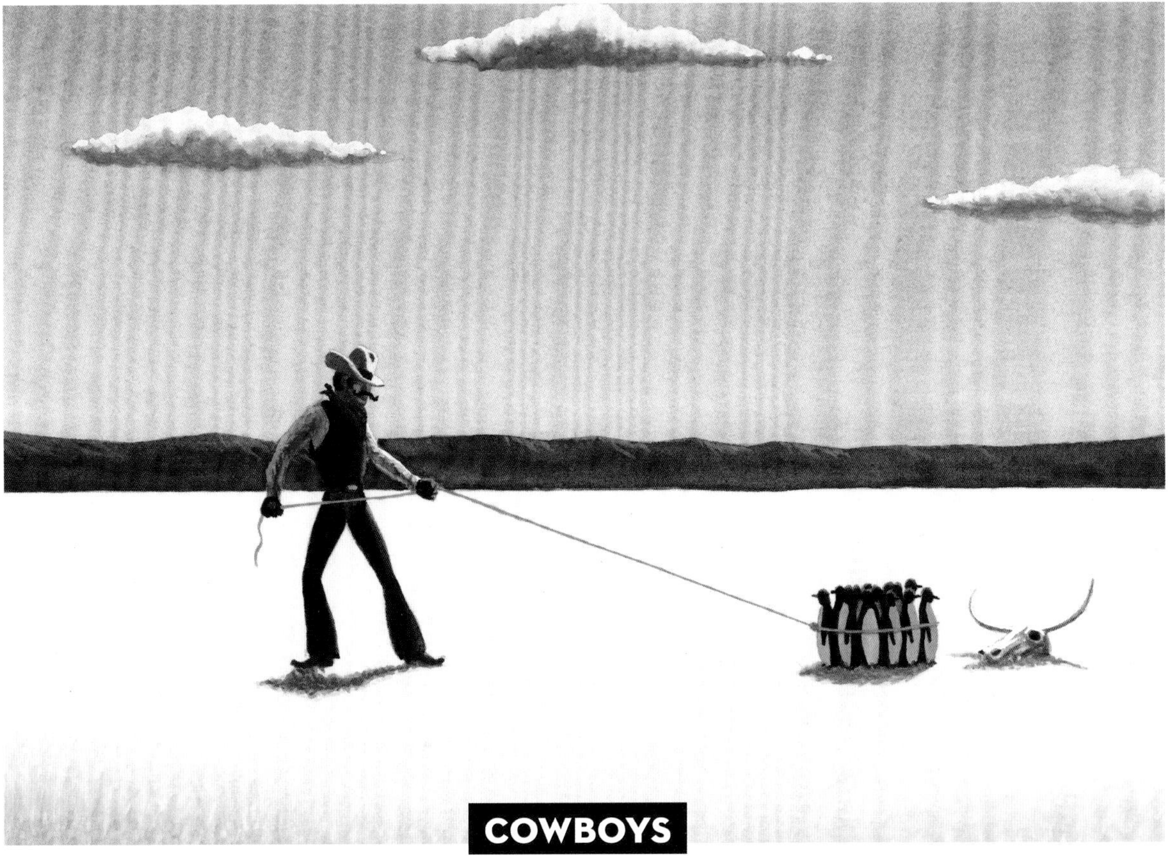

COWBOYS

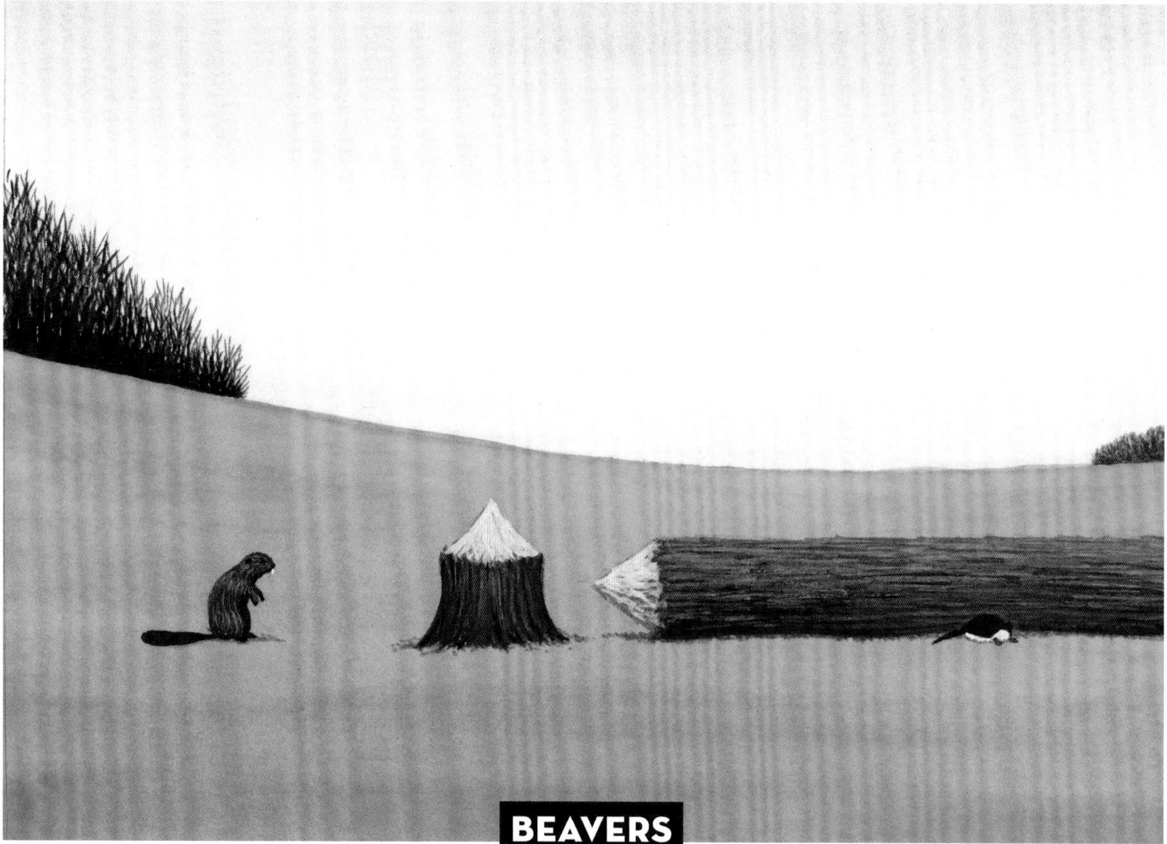

BEAVERS

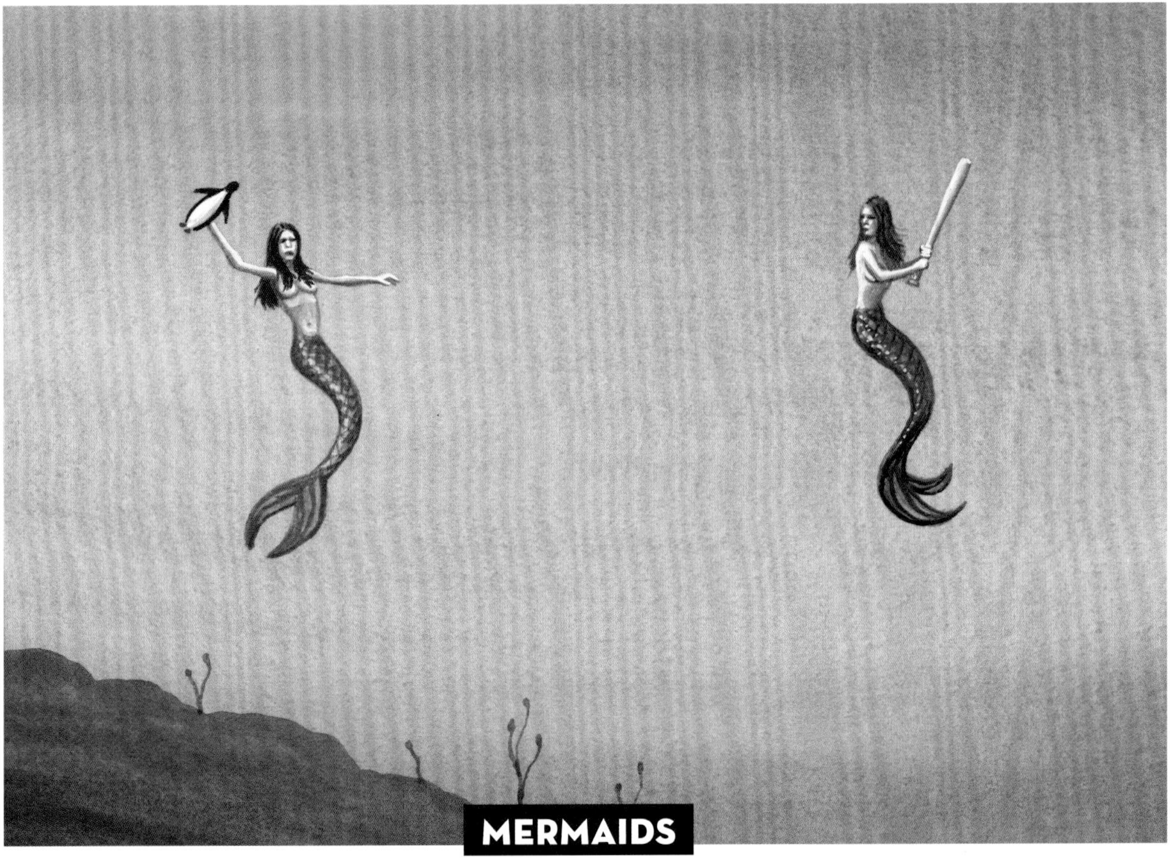

MERMAIDS

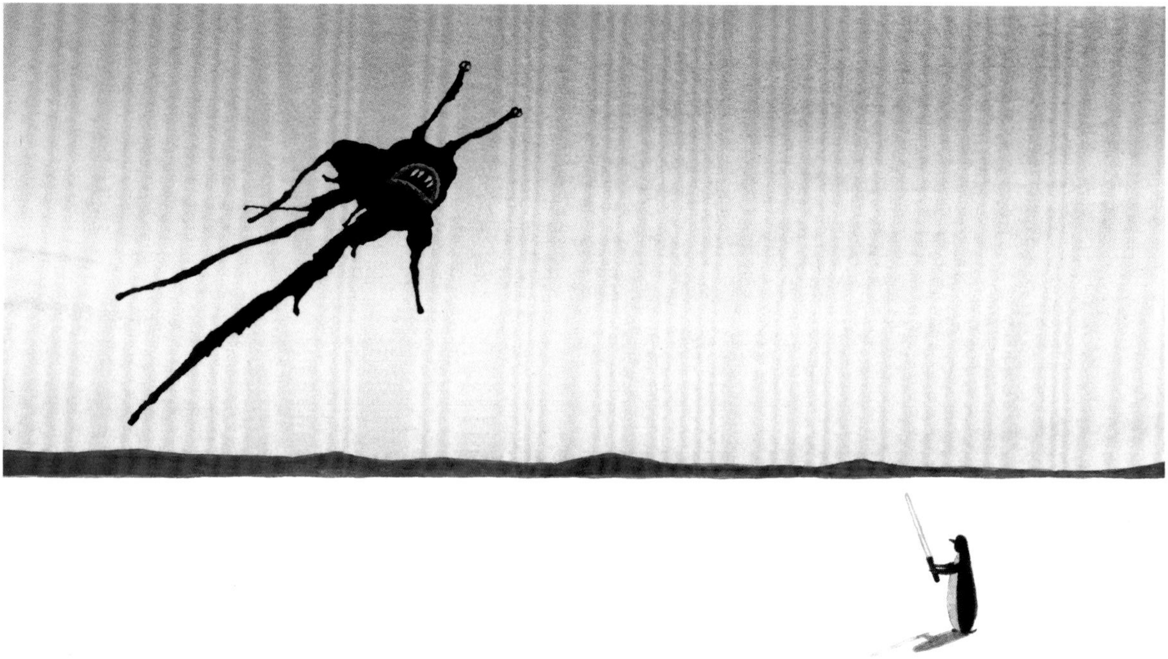

INVASIVE SPECIES

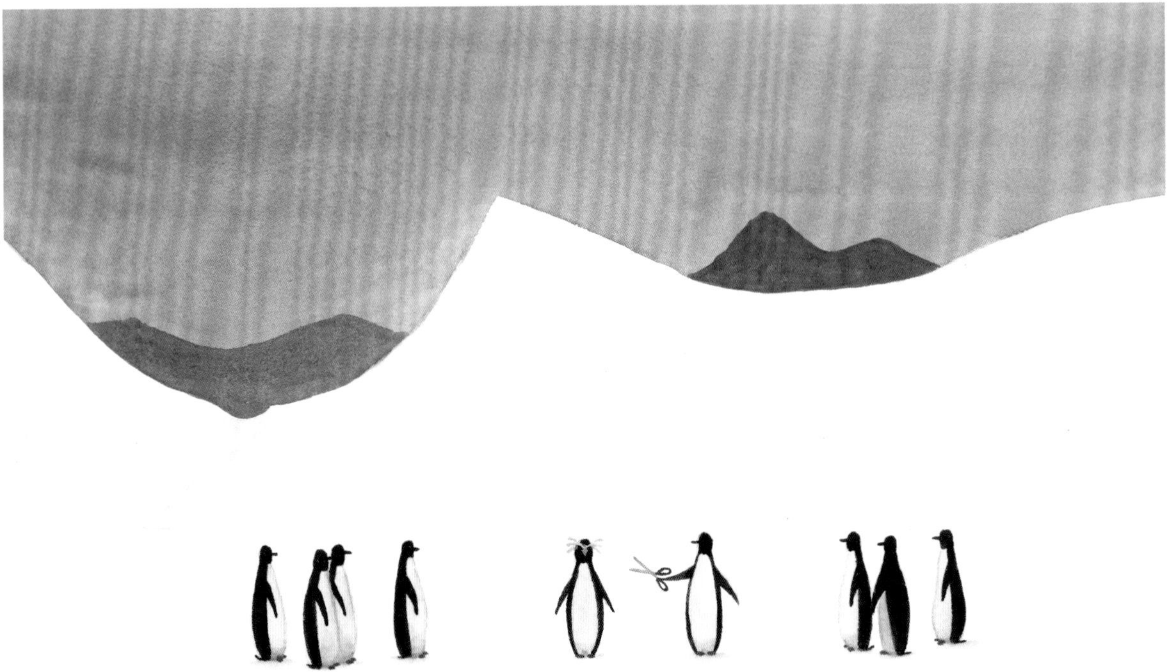

BAD HAIRCUTS

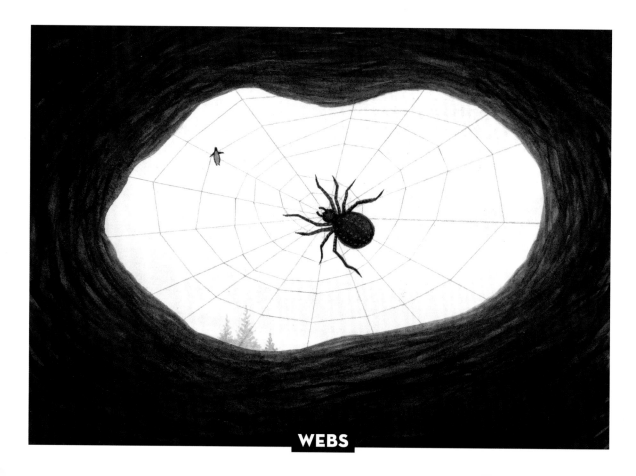

WEBS

SERPENTS

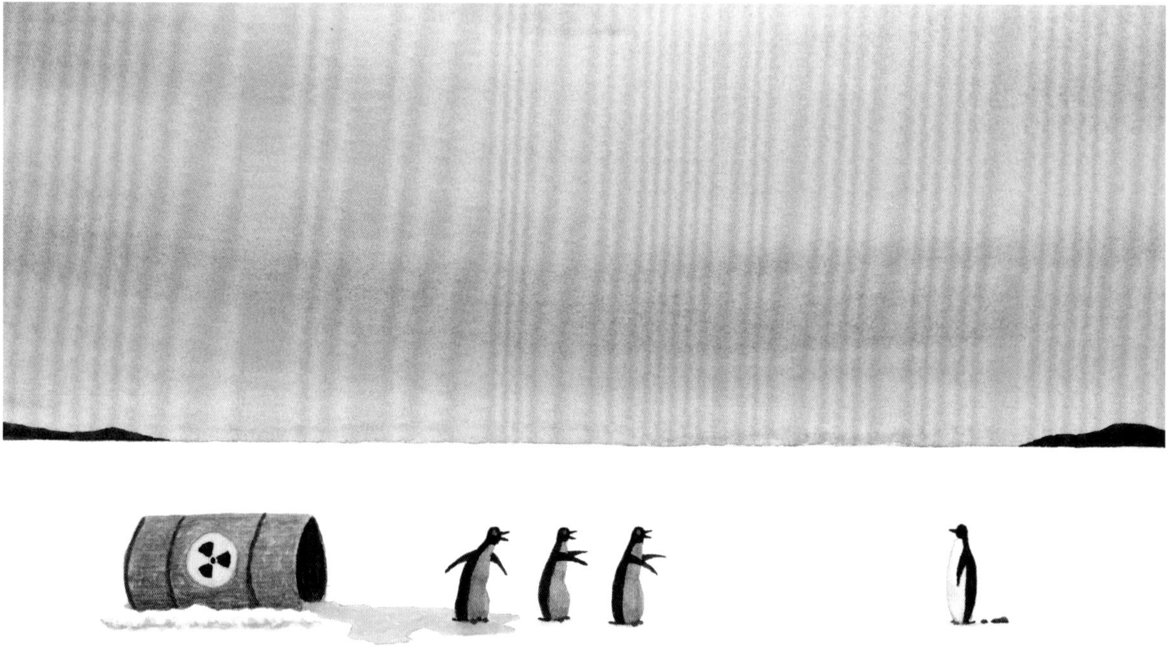

RADIATION-INDUCED ZOMBIISM

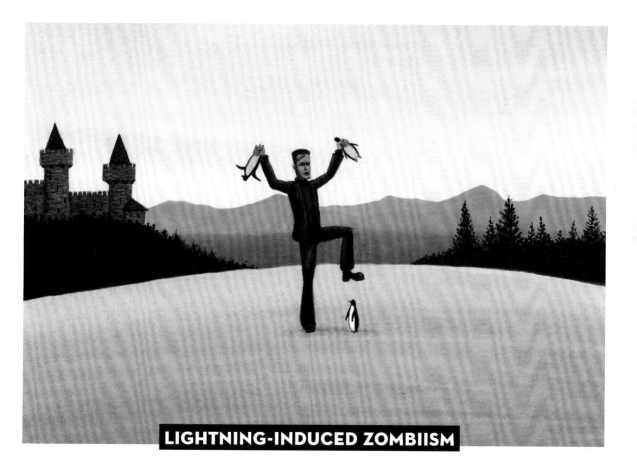

LIGHTNING-INDUCED ZOMBIISM

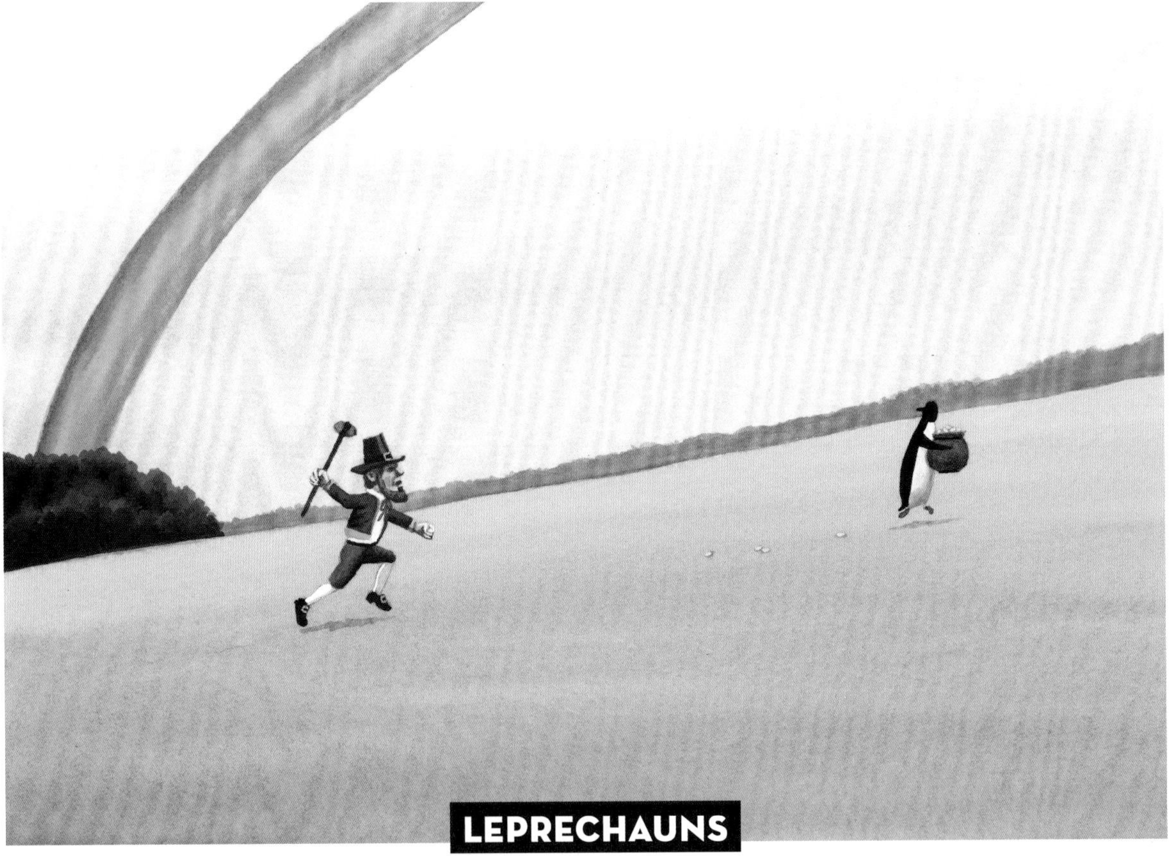

LEPRECHAUNS

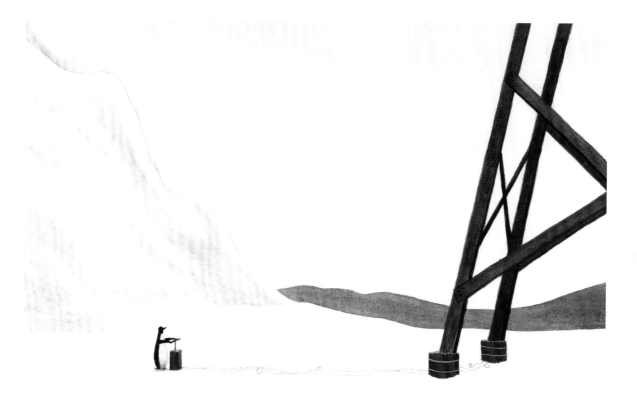

OIL RIGS

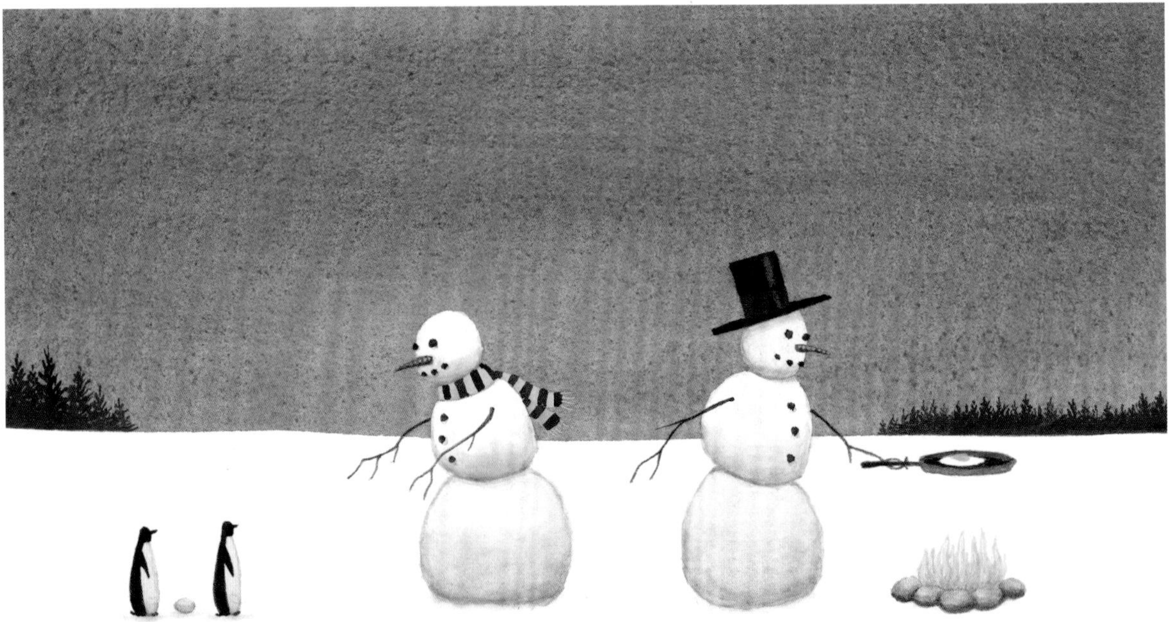

SNOWMEN

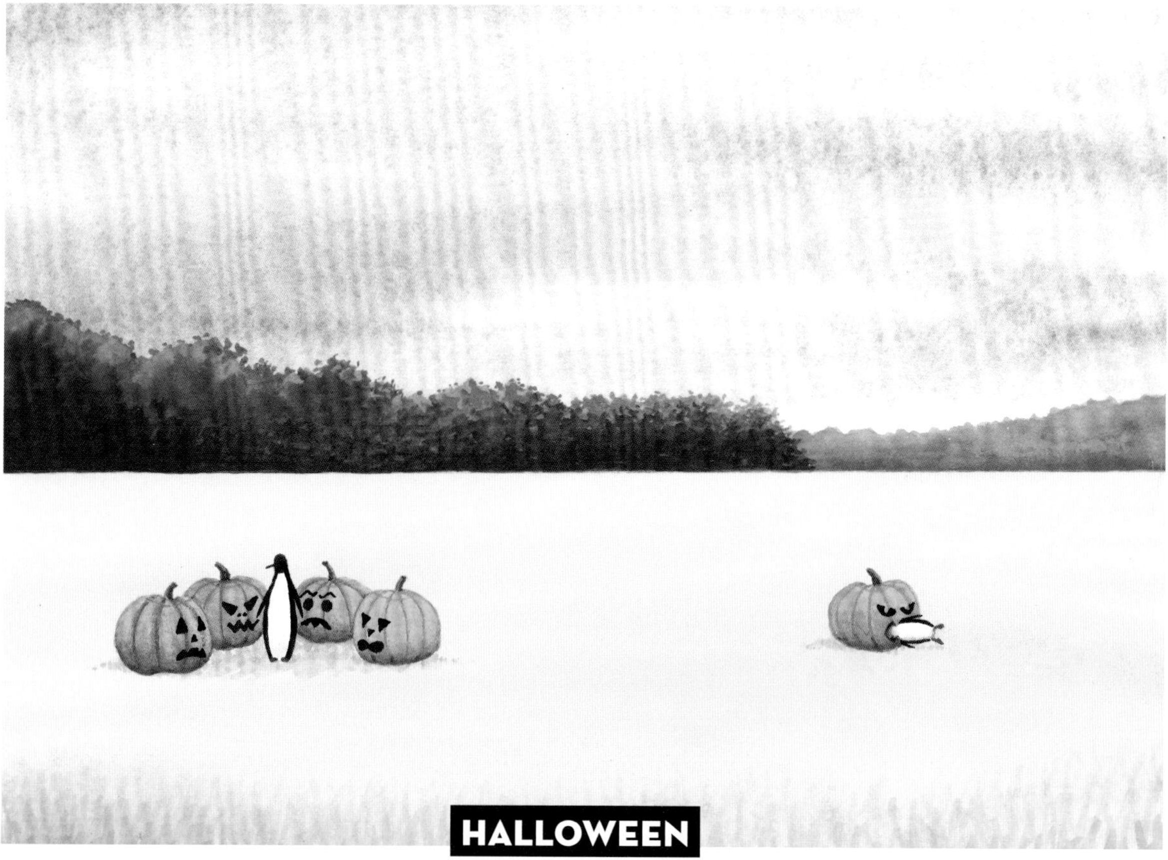

HALLOWEEN

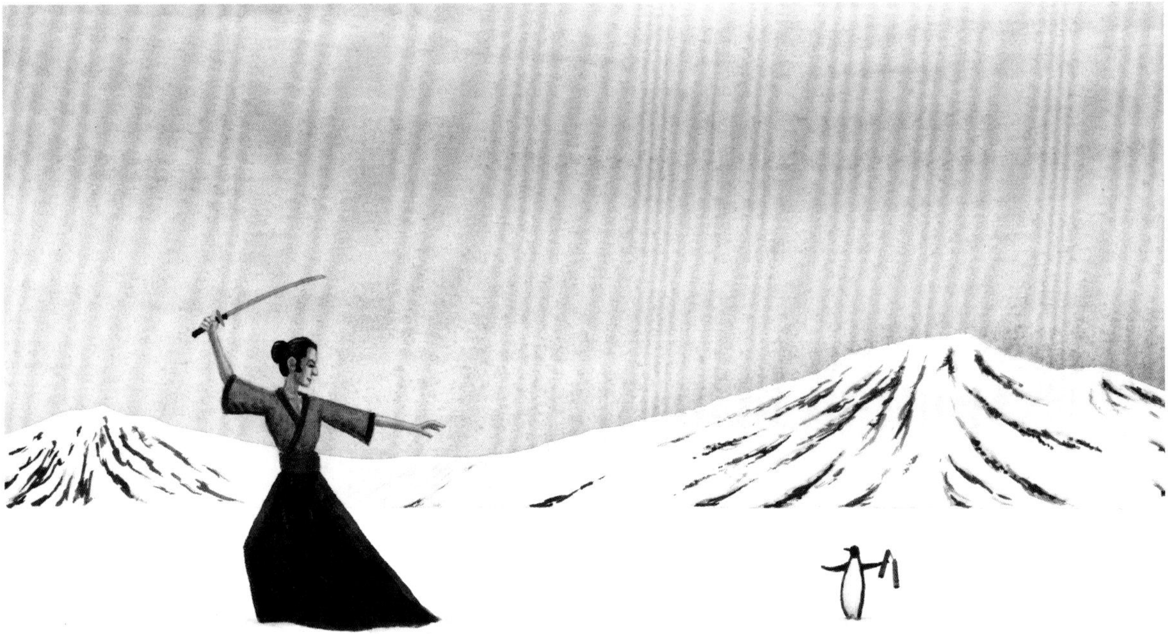

SAMURAI

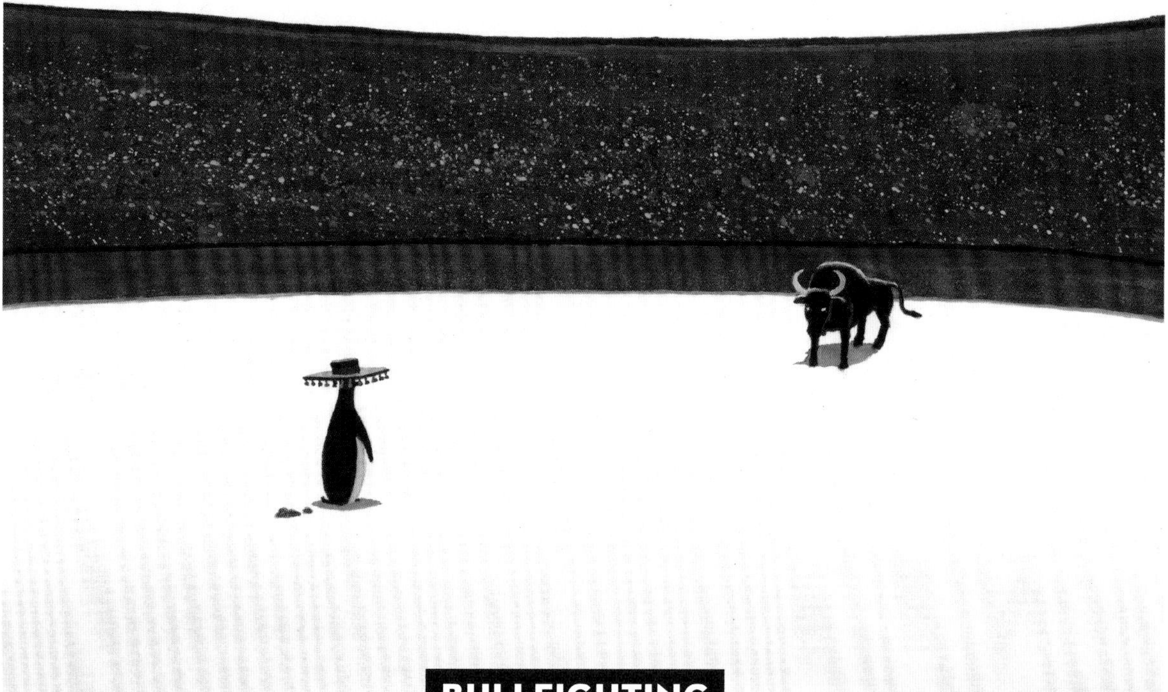

BULLFIGHTING

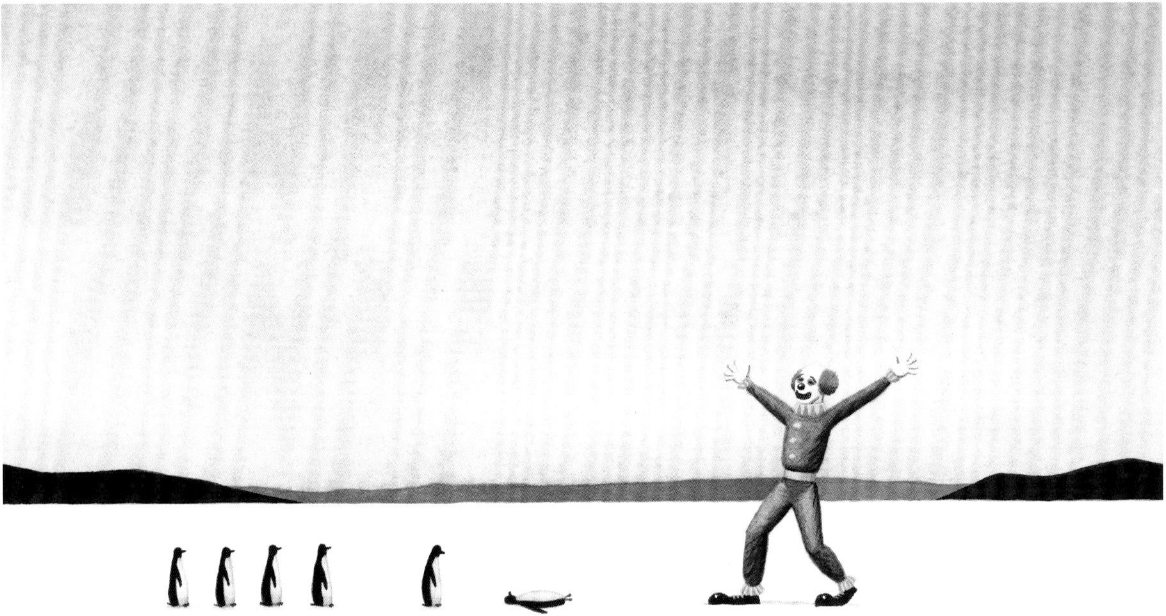

CLOWNS

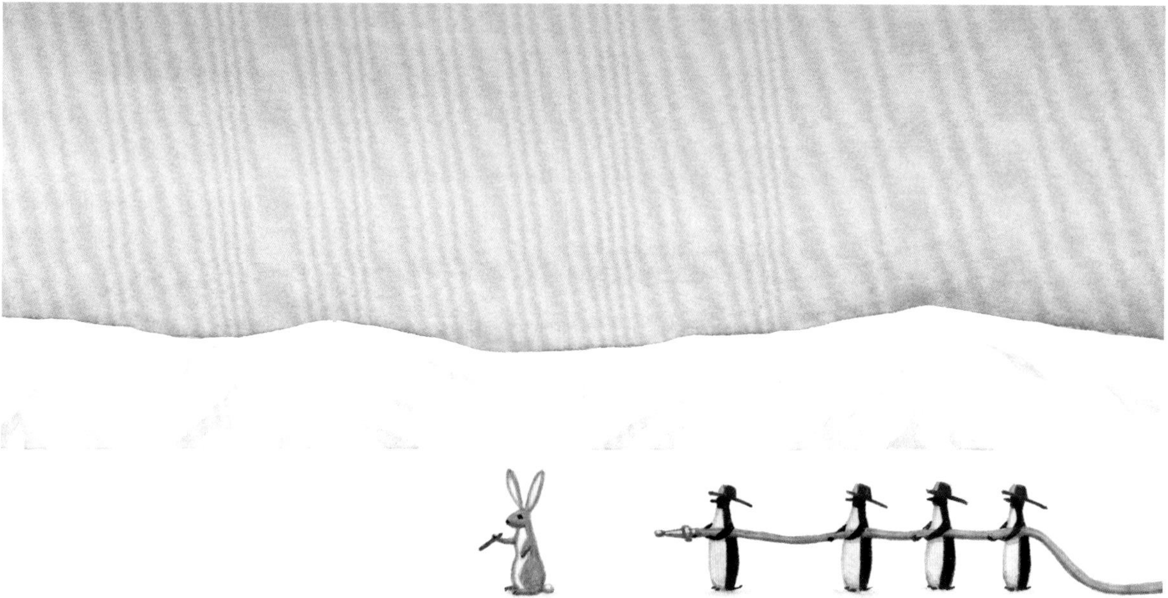

CIGARS

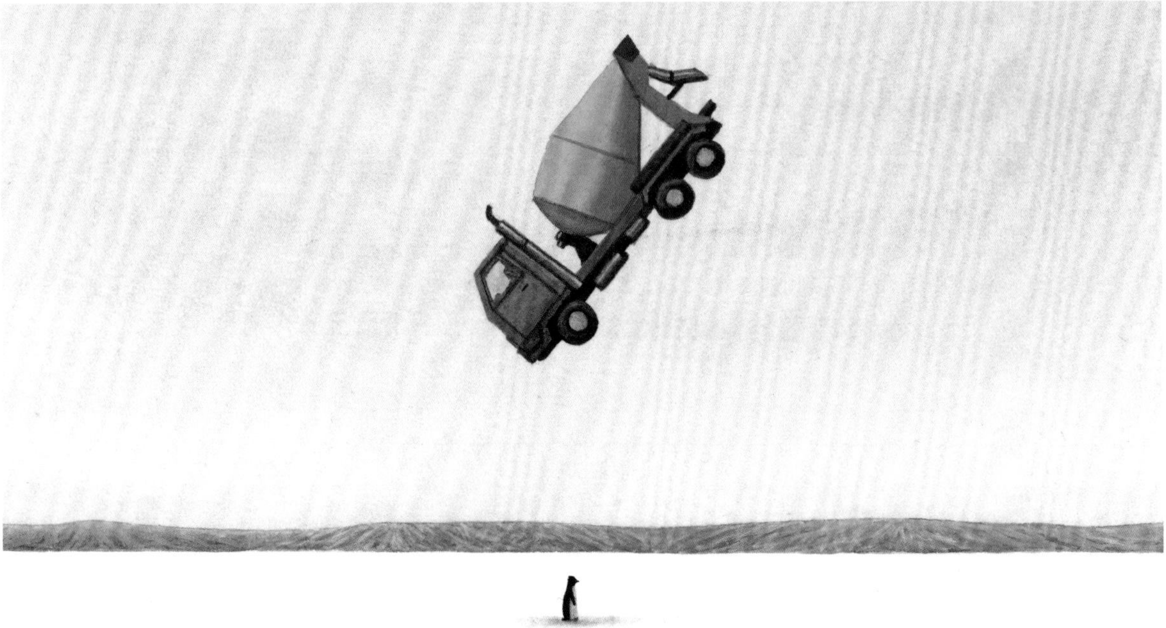

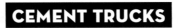

CEMENT TRUCKS

PENGUINS REALLY LIKE...

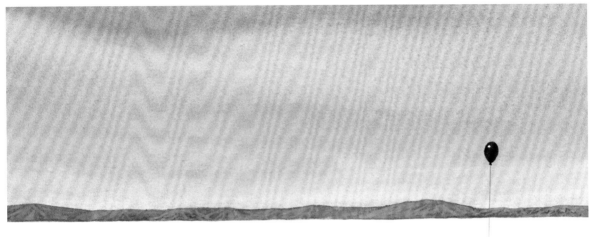

BALLOONS

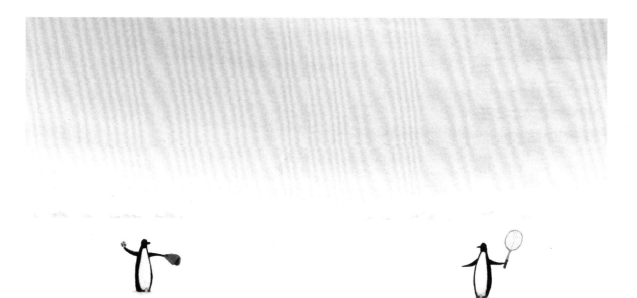

SPORTS

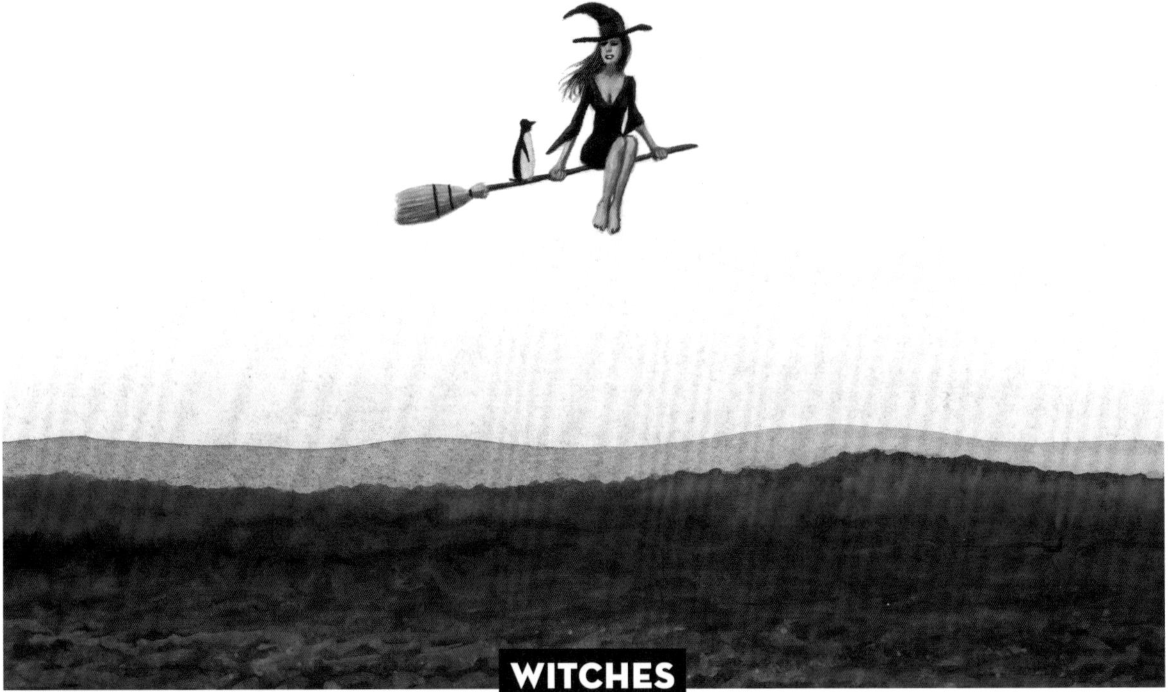

WITCHES

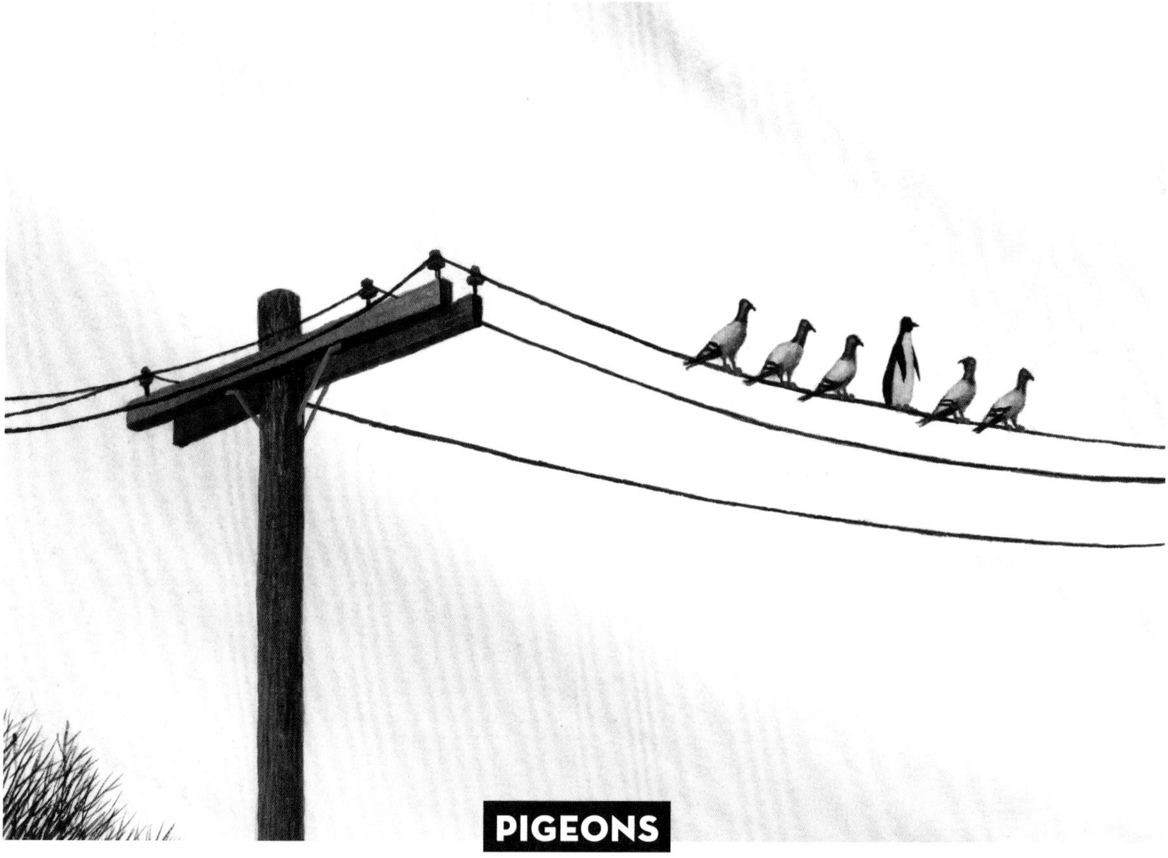

PIGEONS

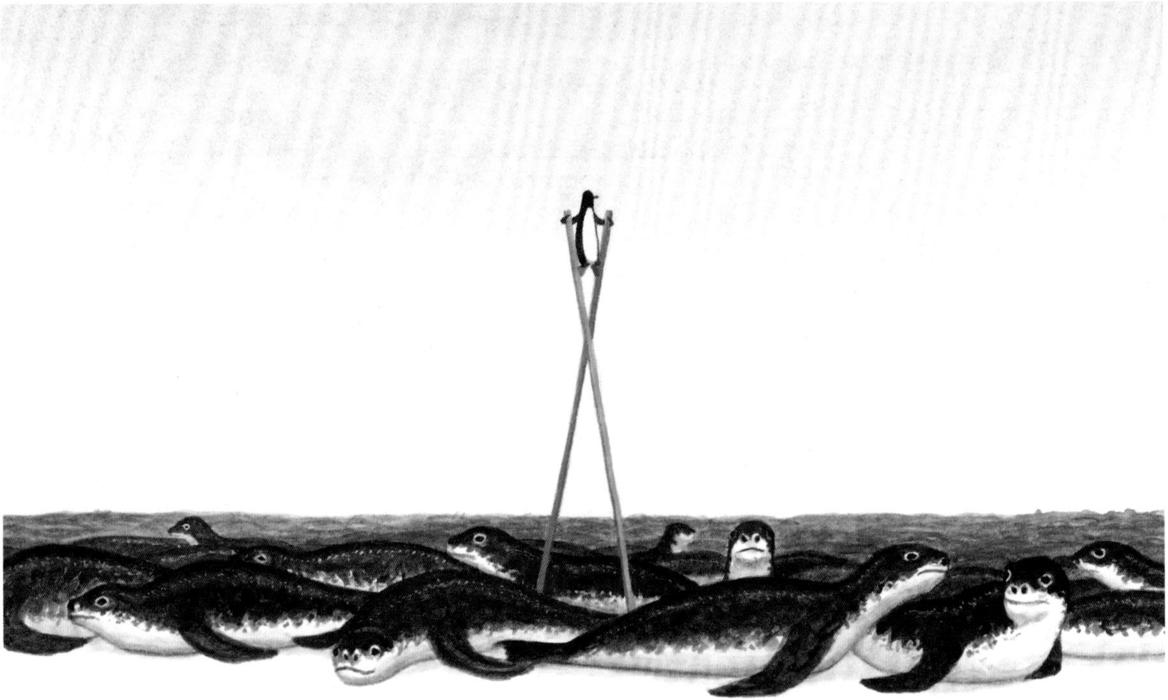

STILTS

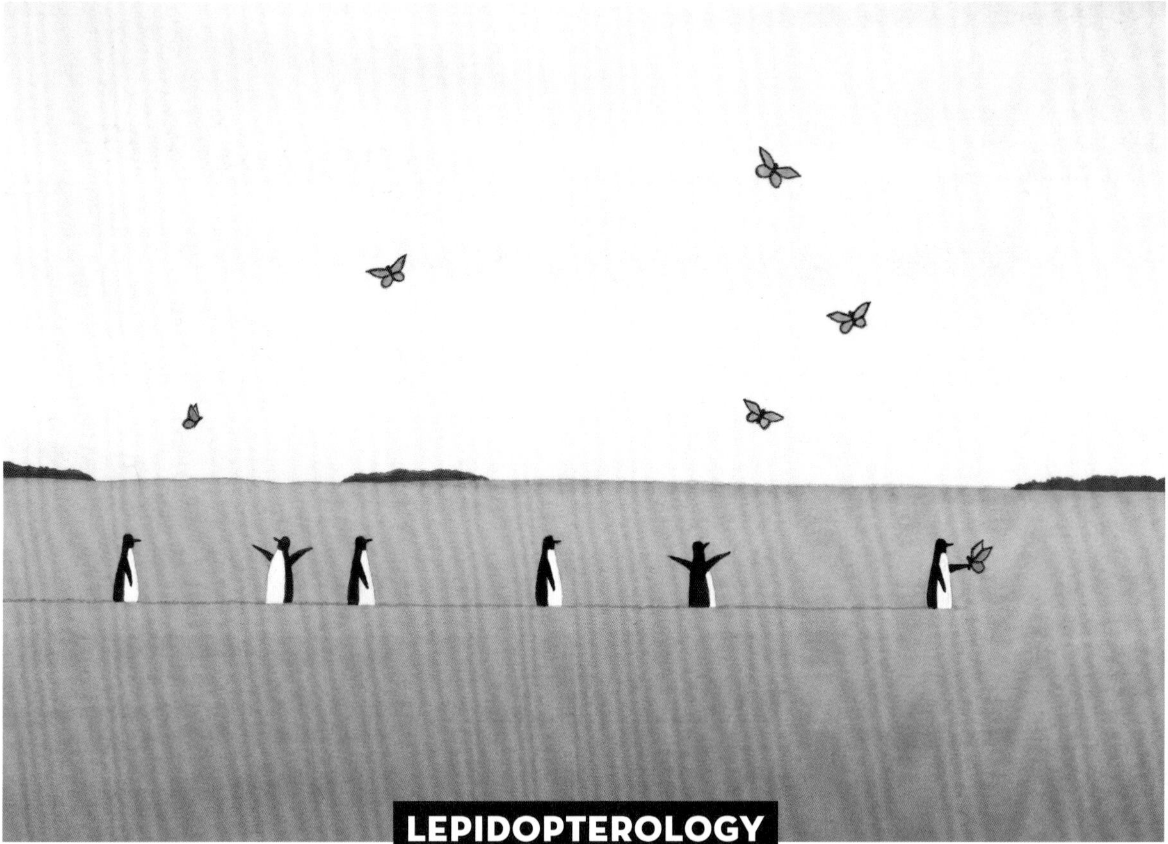

LEPIDOPTEROLOGY

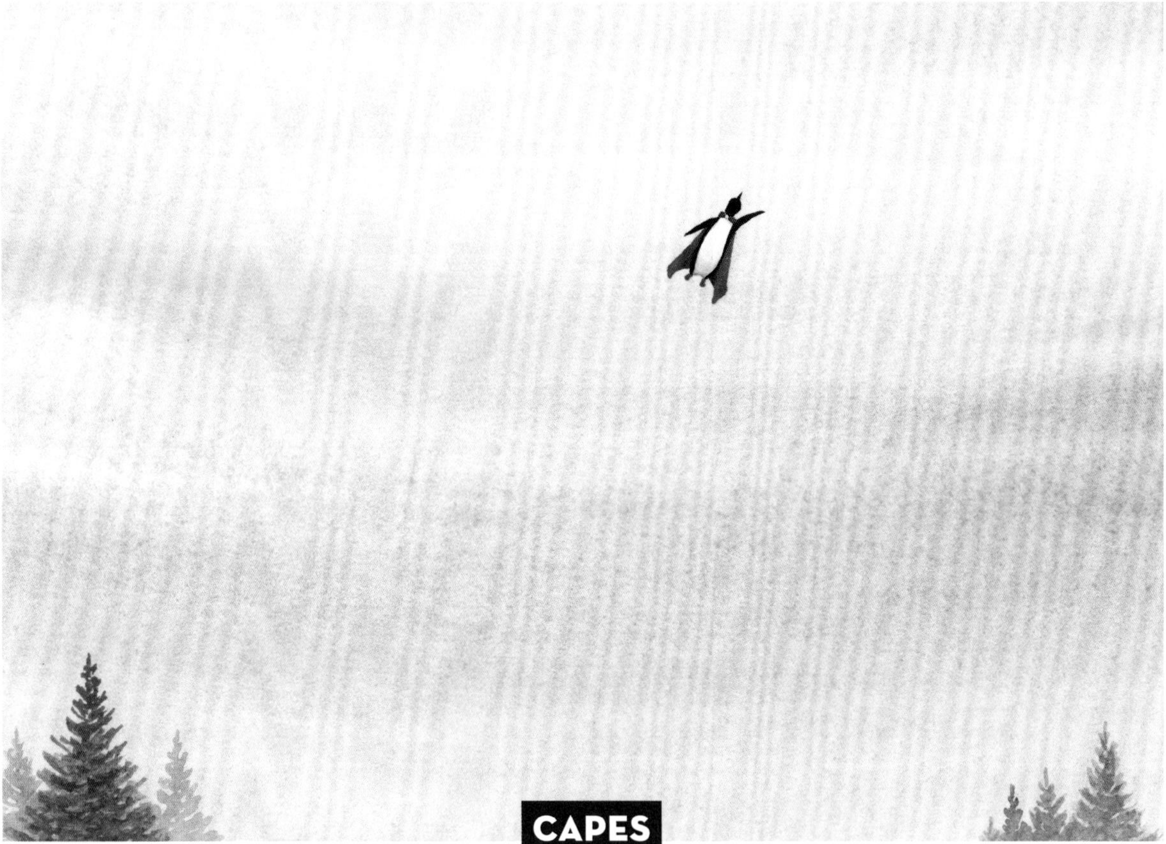

CAPES

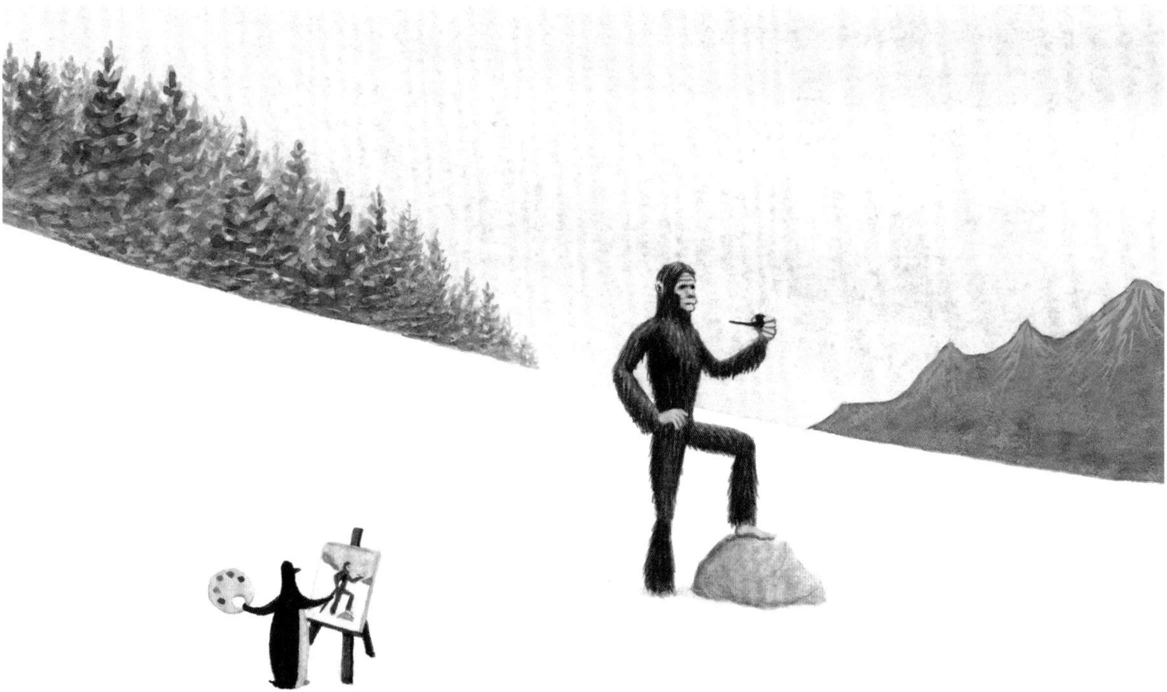

PORTRAITURE

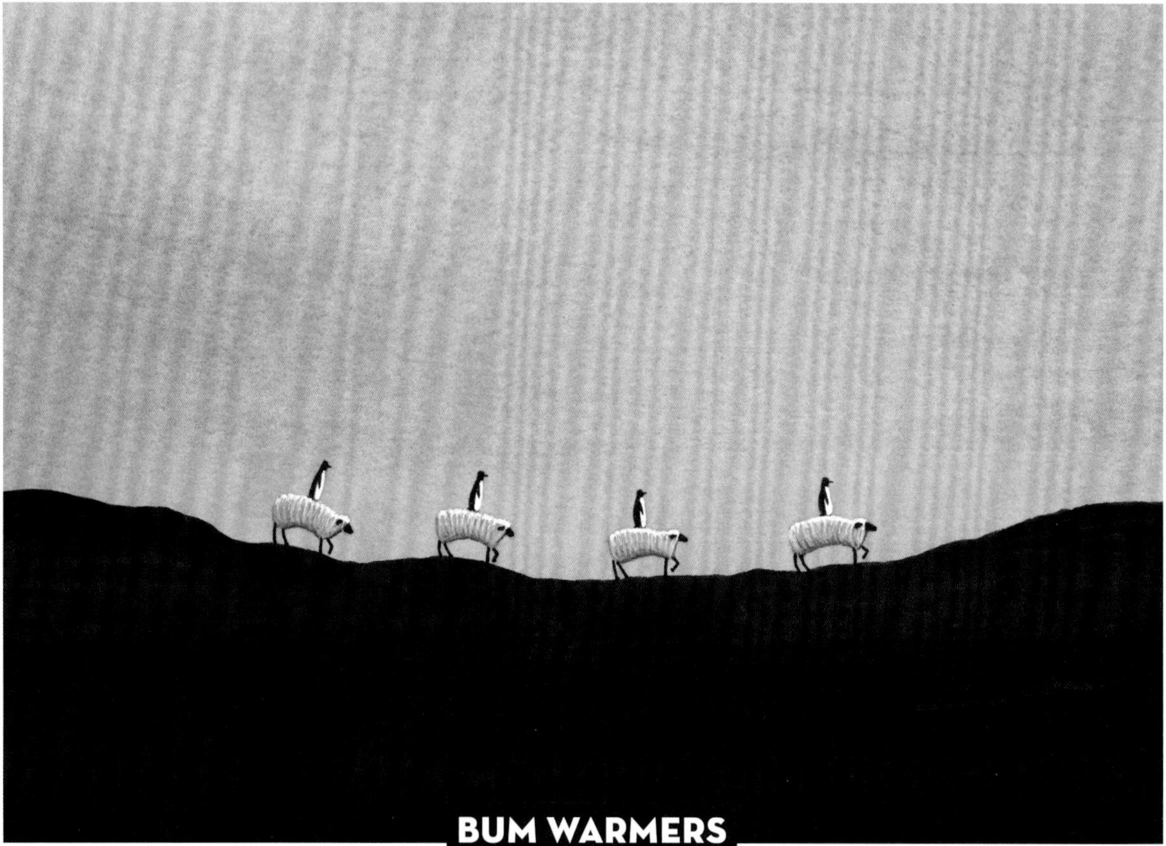

BUM WARMERS

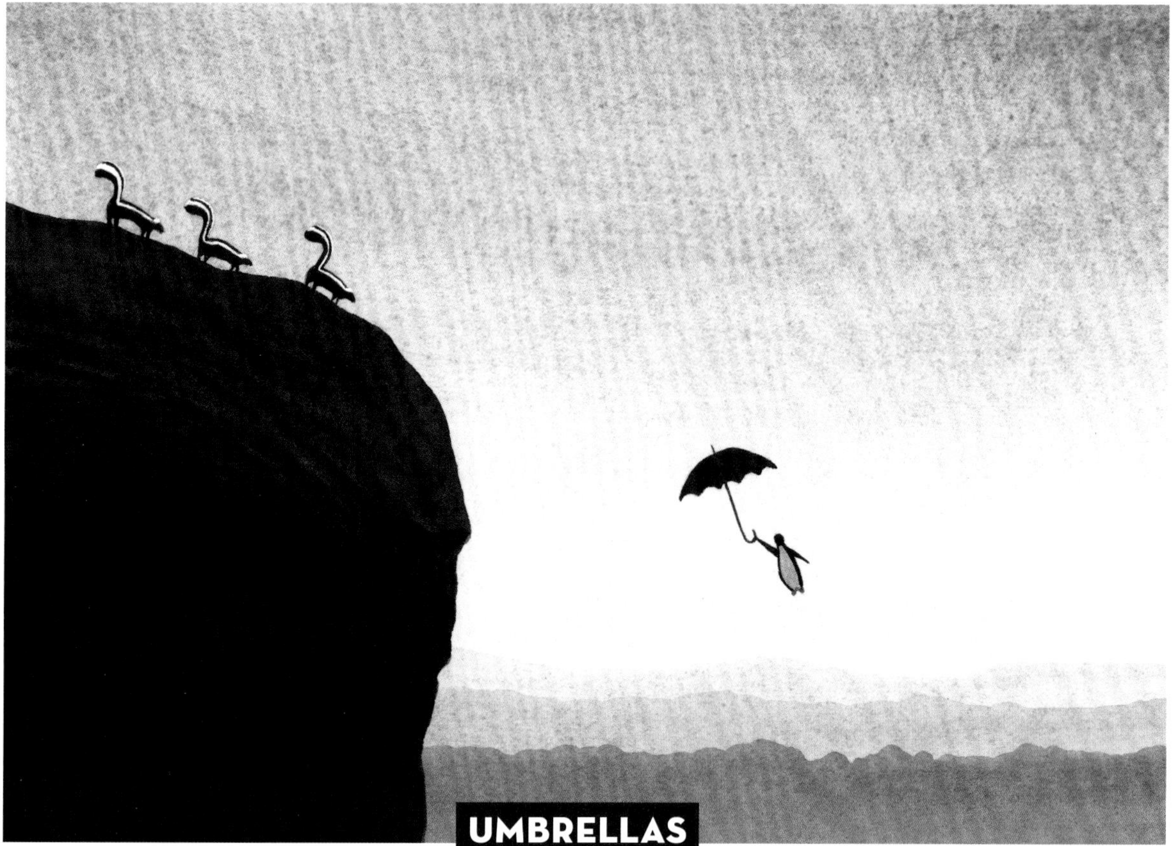

UMBRELLAS

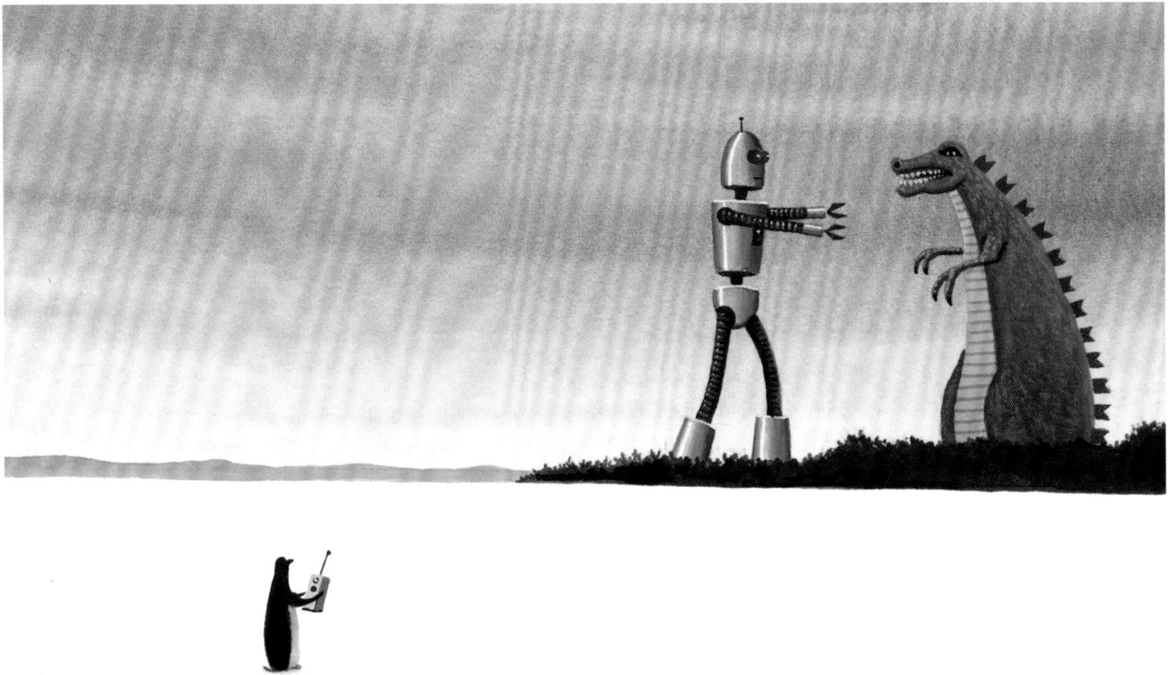

REMOTE CONTROLS

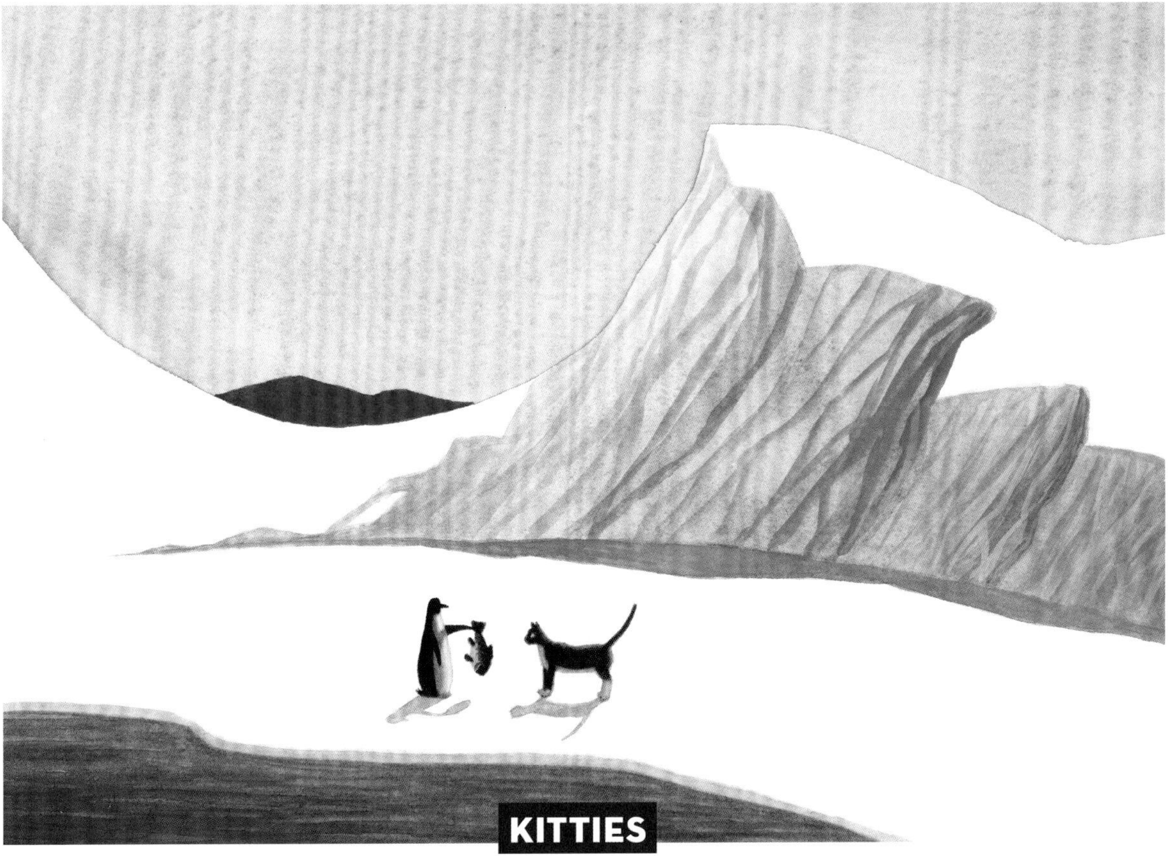
KITTIES

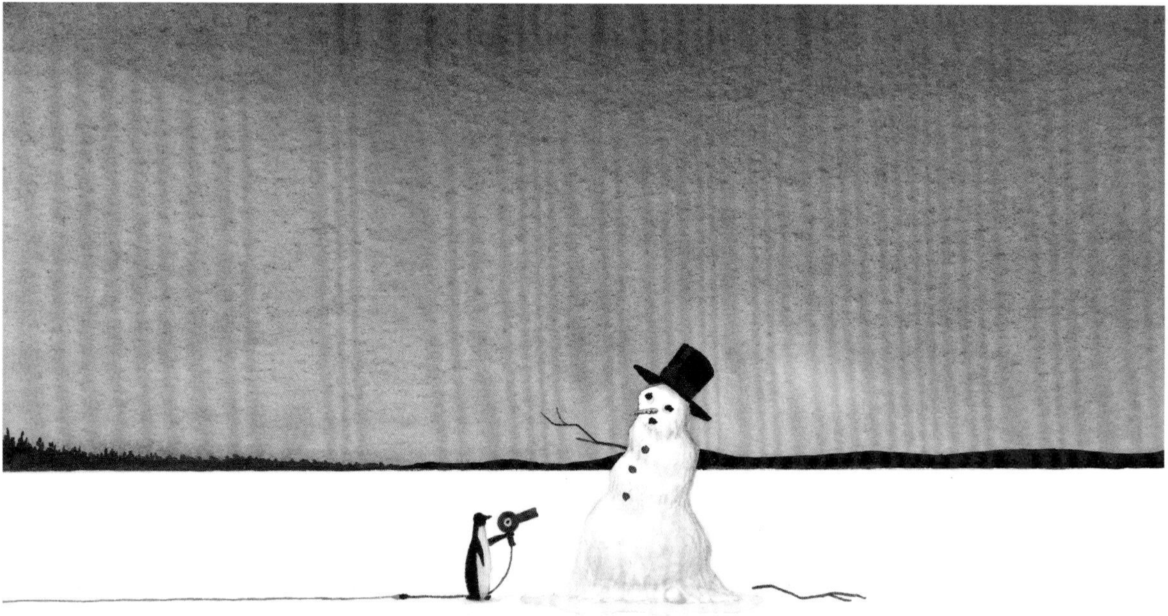

GETTING EVEN

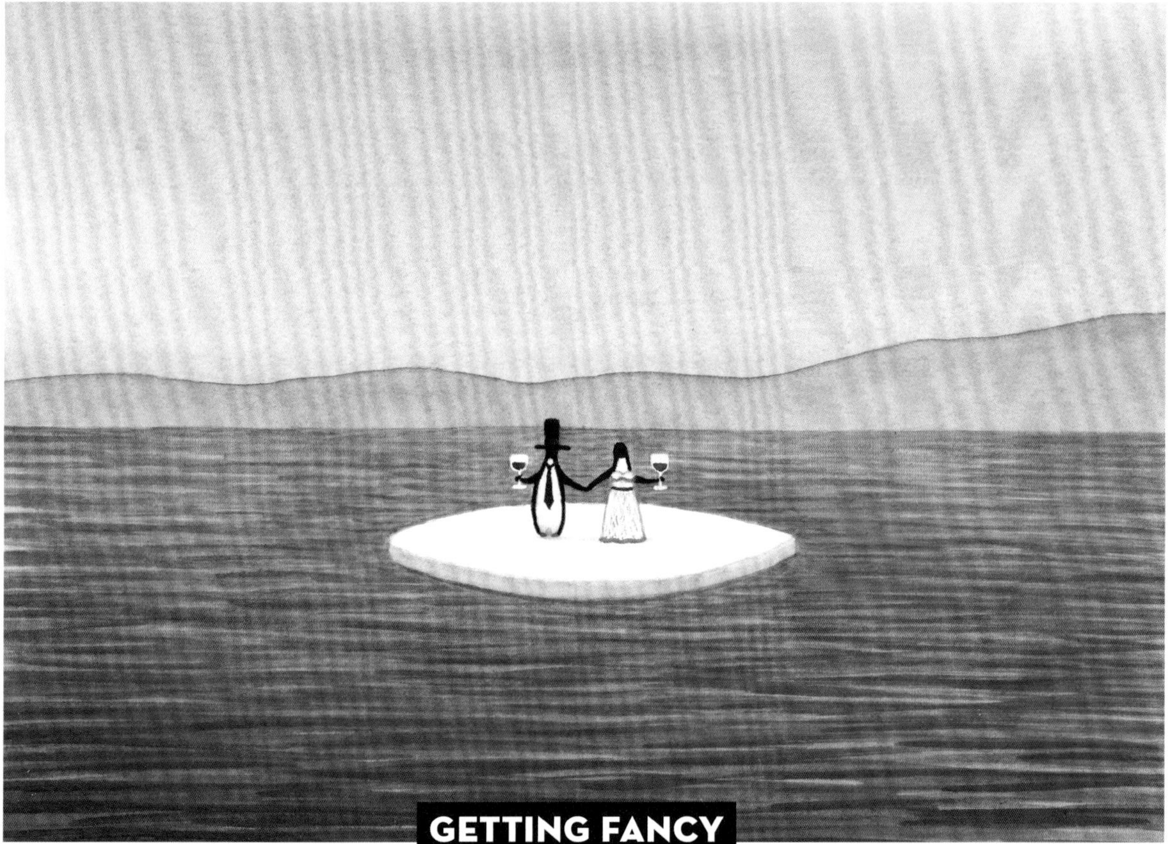

GETTING FANCY

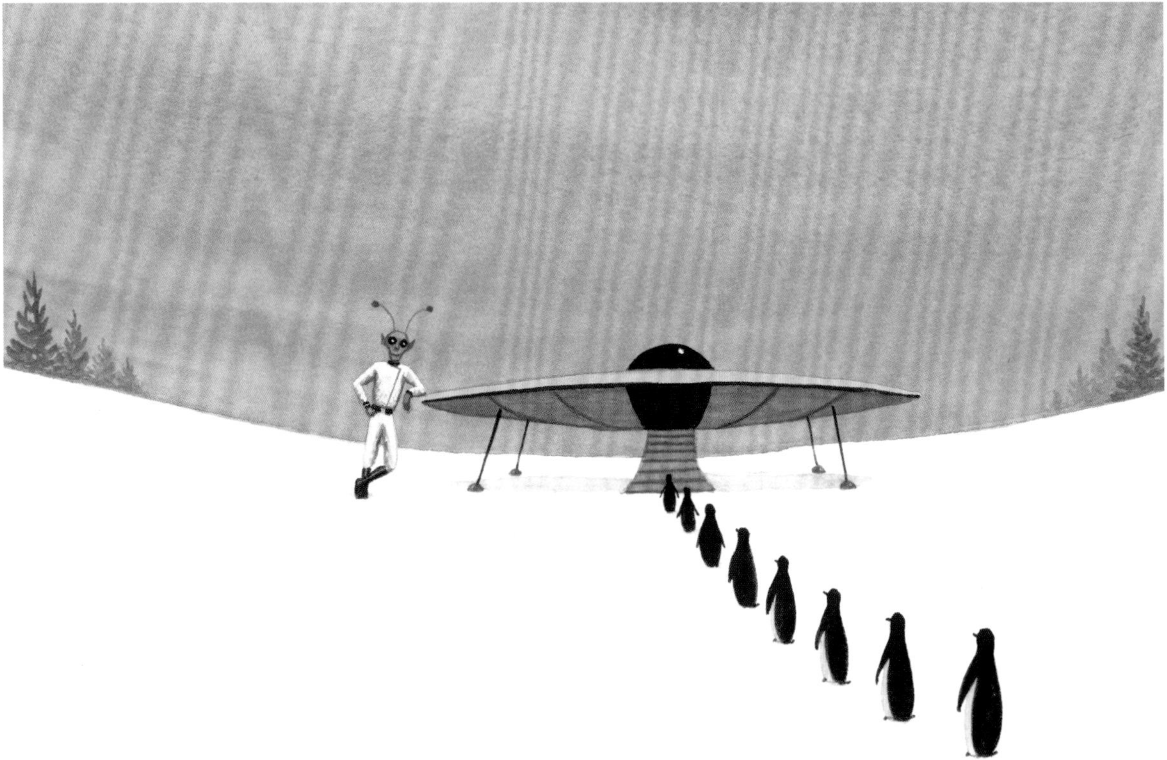

FREE VACATIONS

MOON PENGUINS HATE . . .

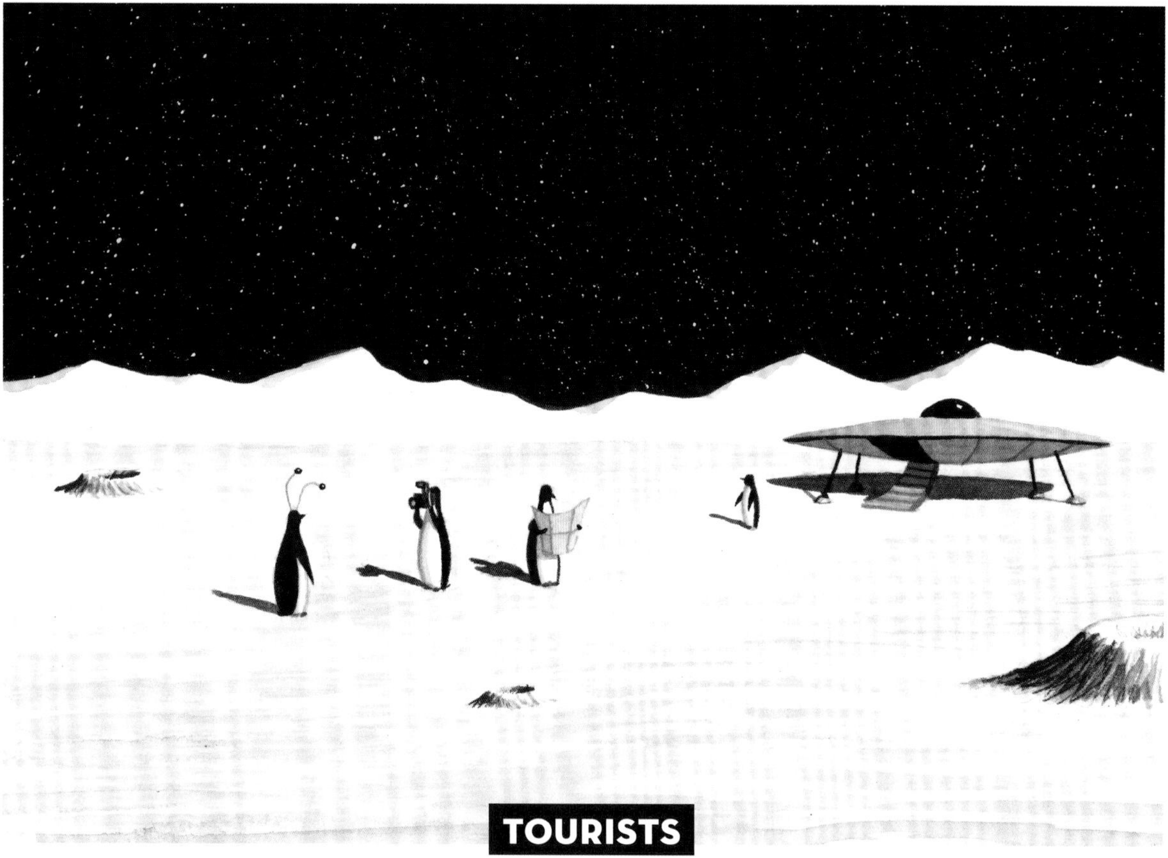

TOURISTS

PENGUINS REALLY HATE...

POORLY CONSTRUCTED STILTS

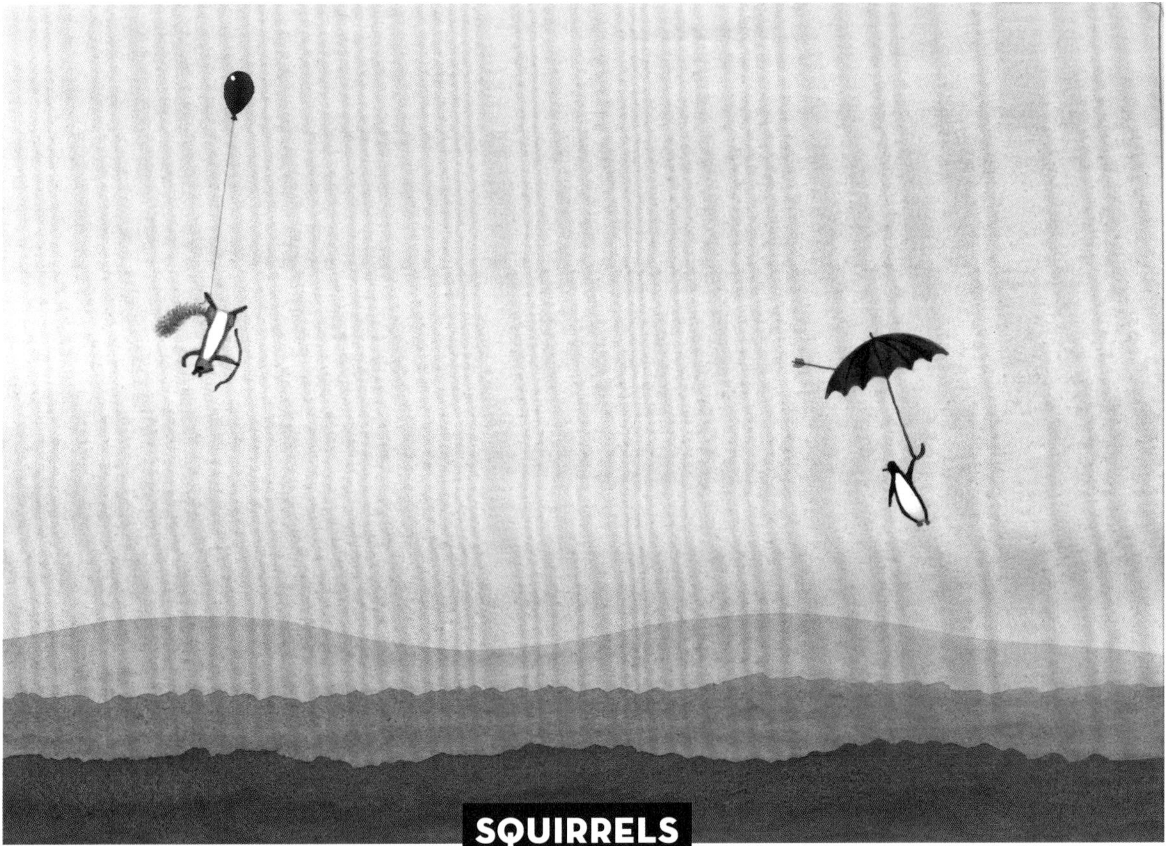

SQUIRRELS

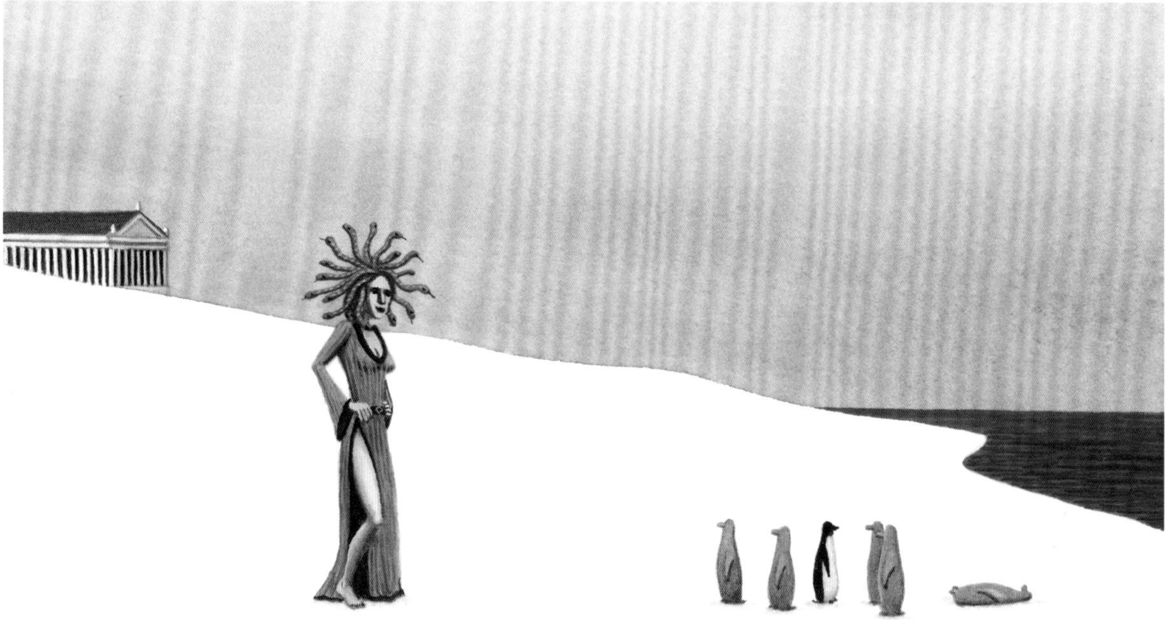

MEDUSA

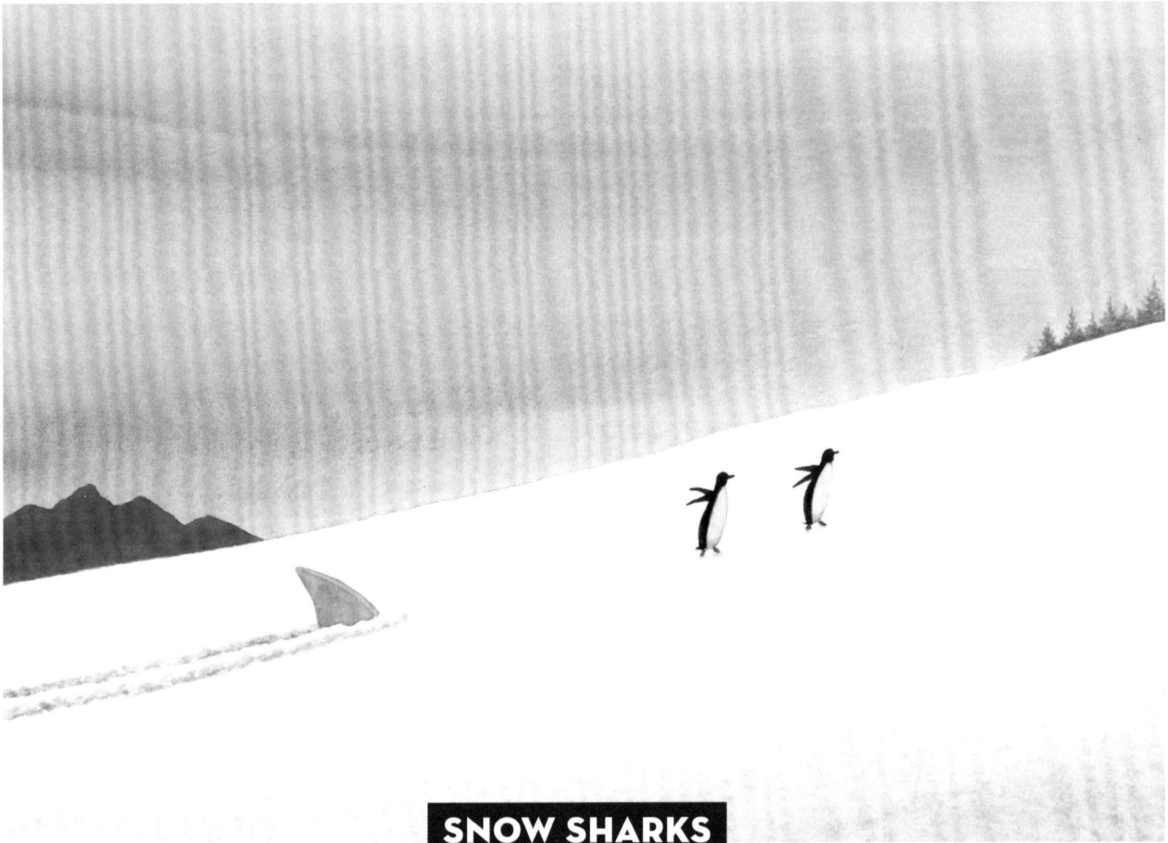

SNOW SHARKS

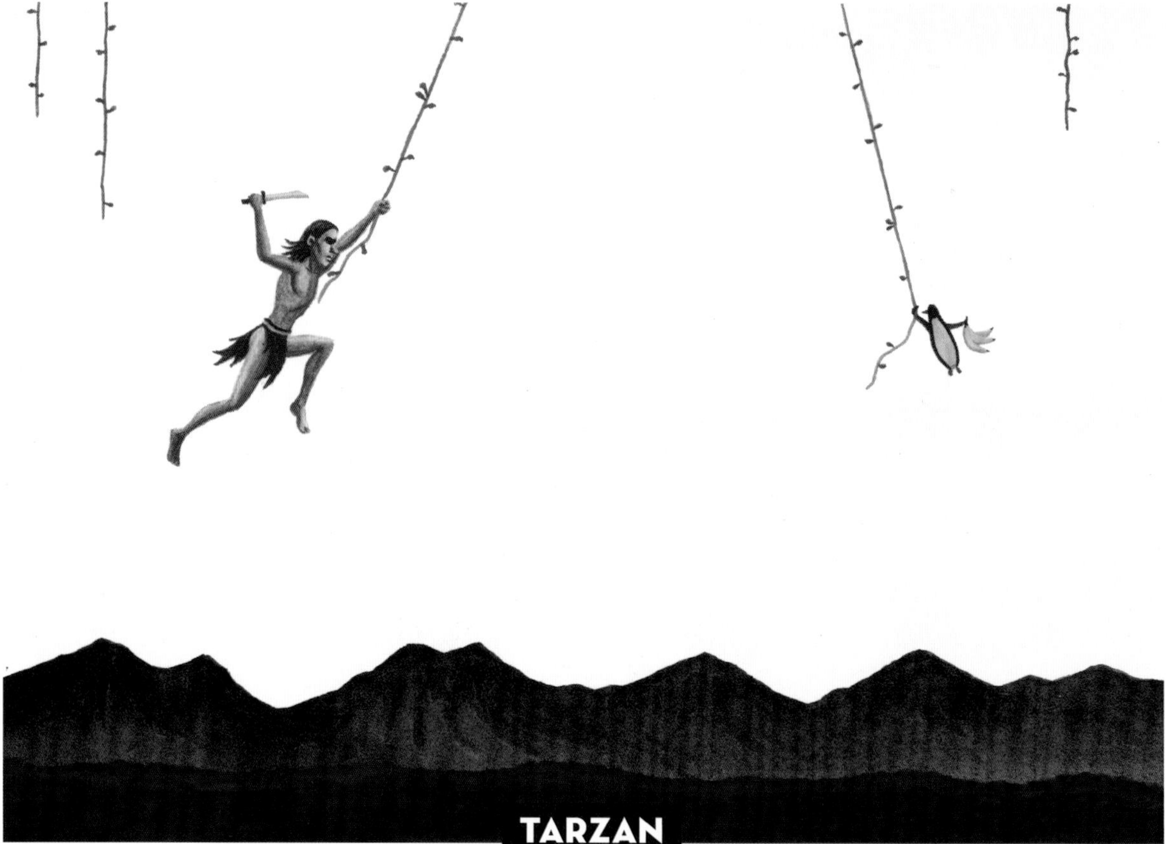

TARZAN

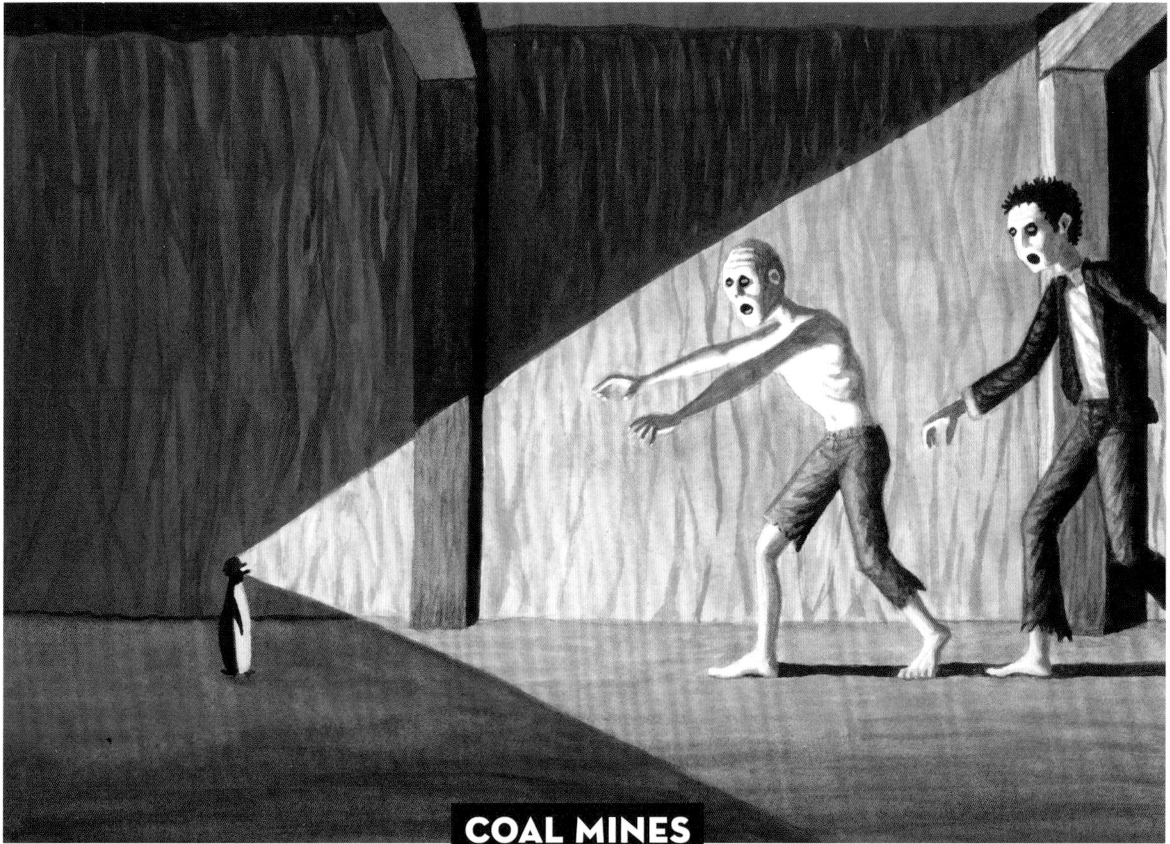

COAL MINES

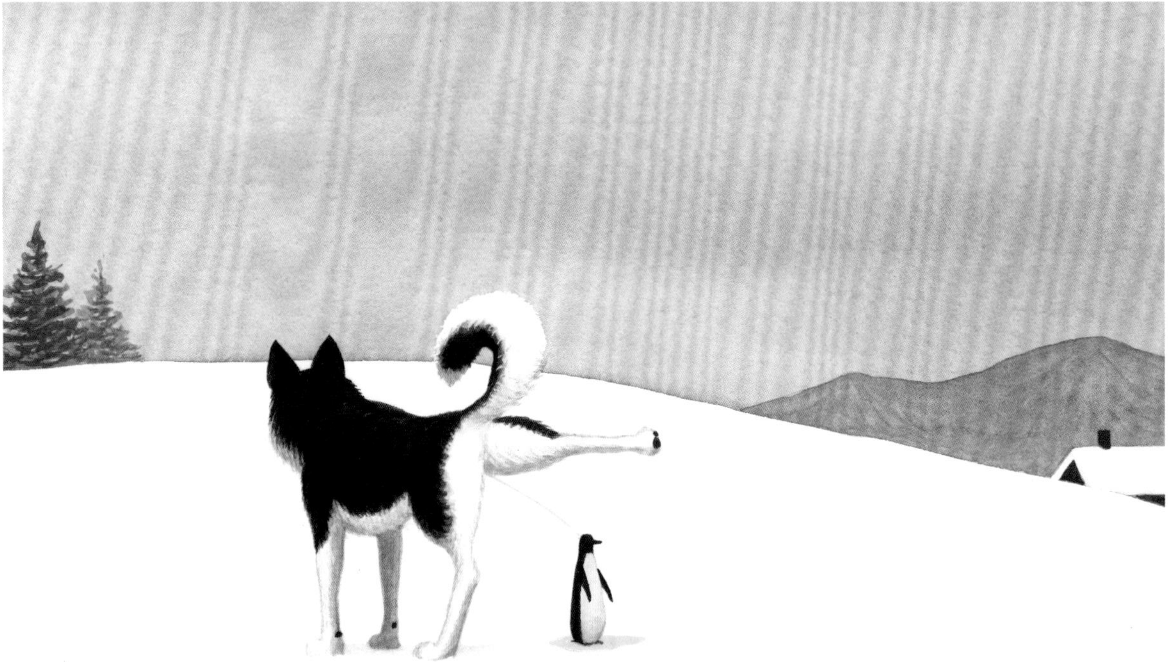

DOGS

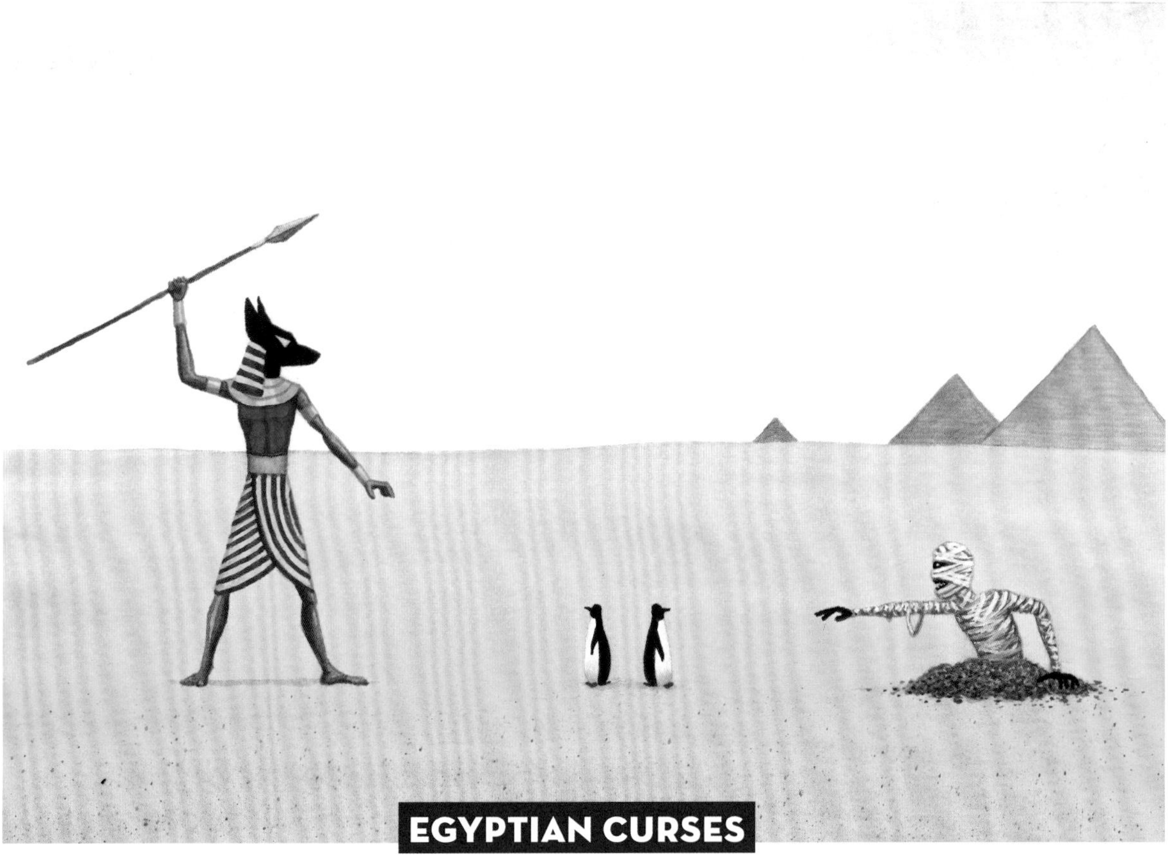

EGYPTIAN CURSES

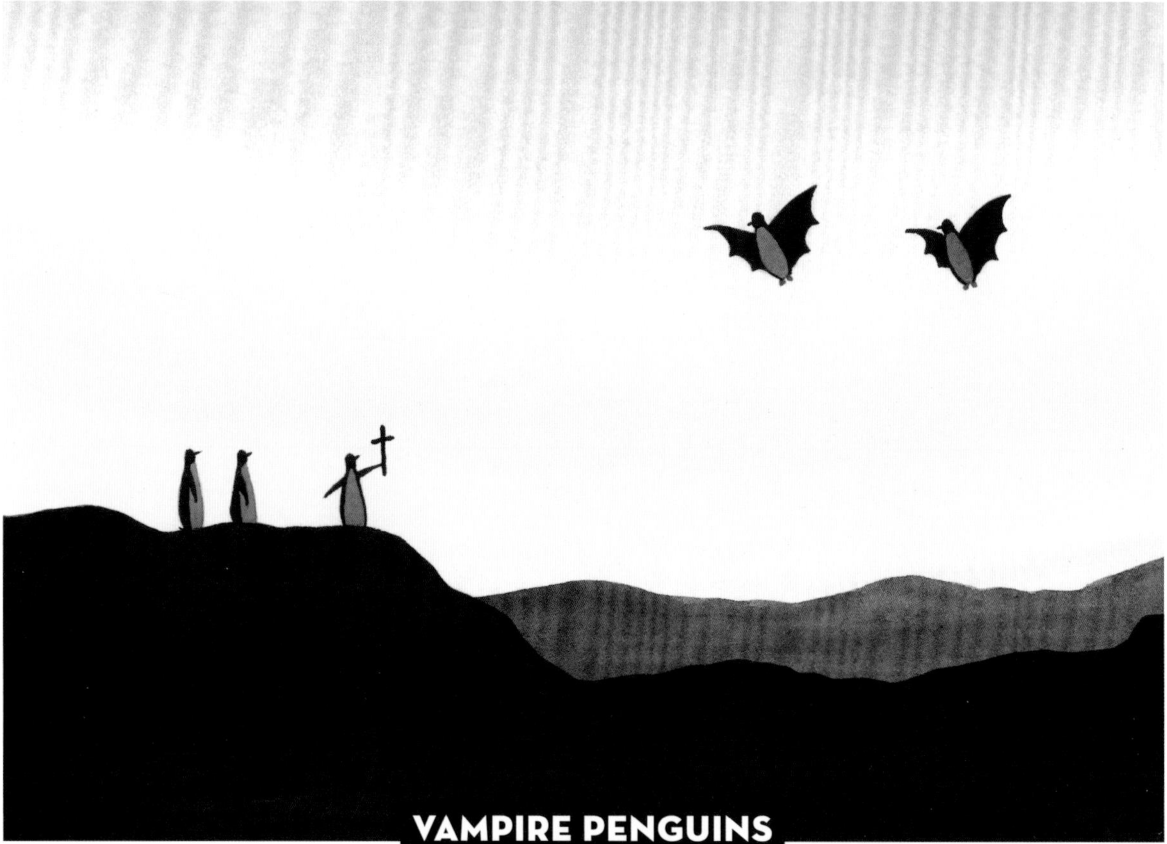

VAMPIRE PENGUINS

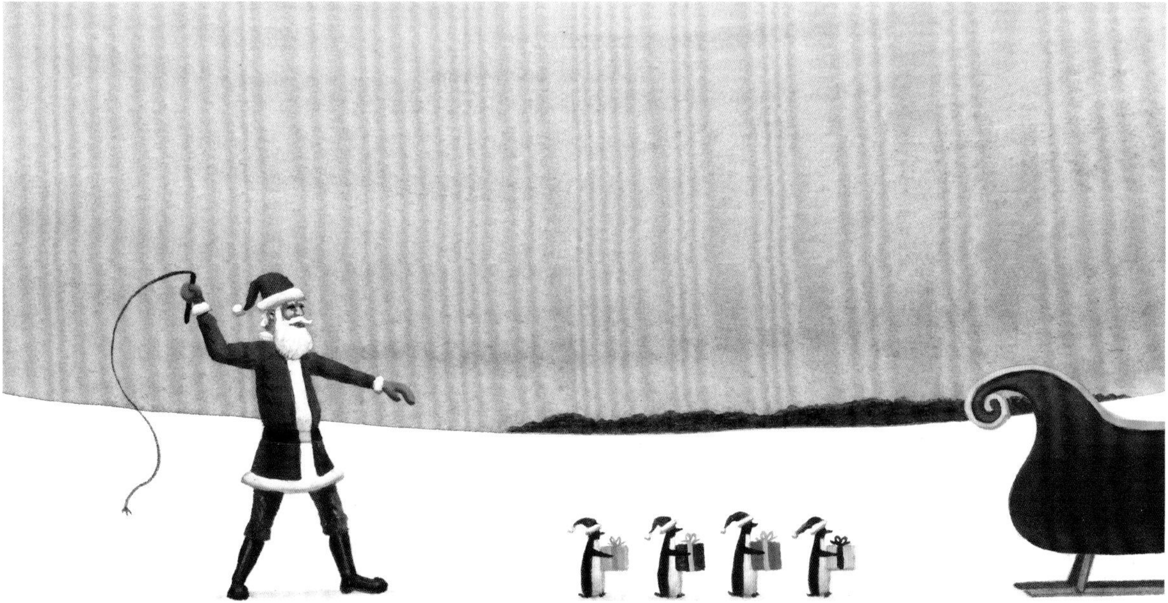

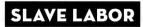

SLAVE LABOR

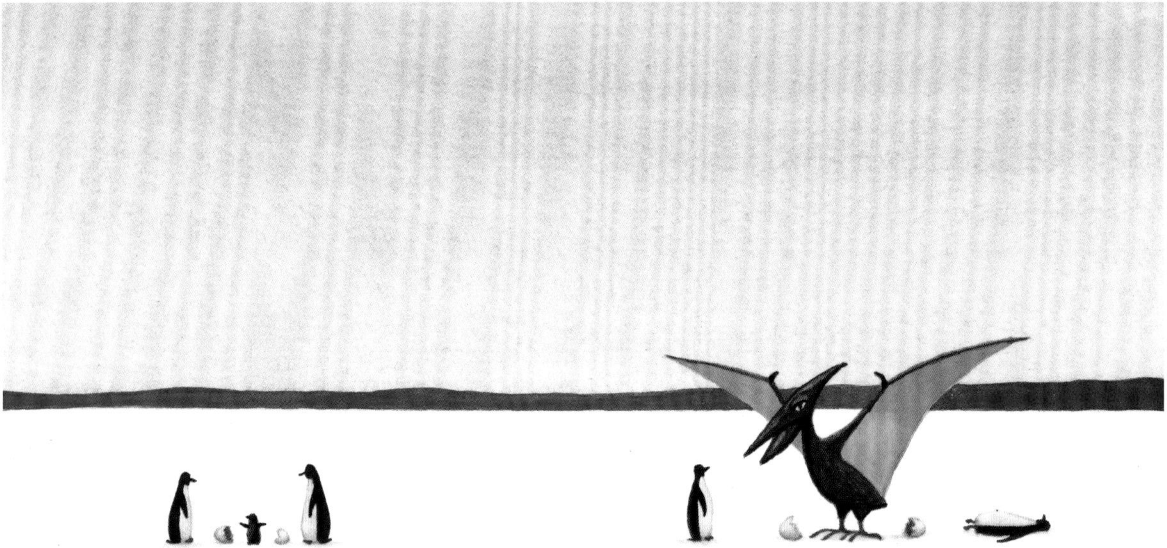

IMPOSTERS

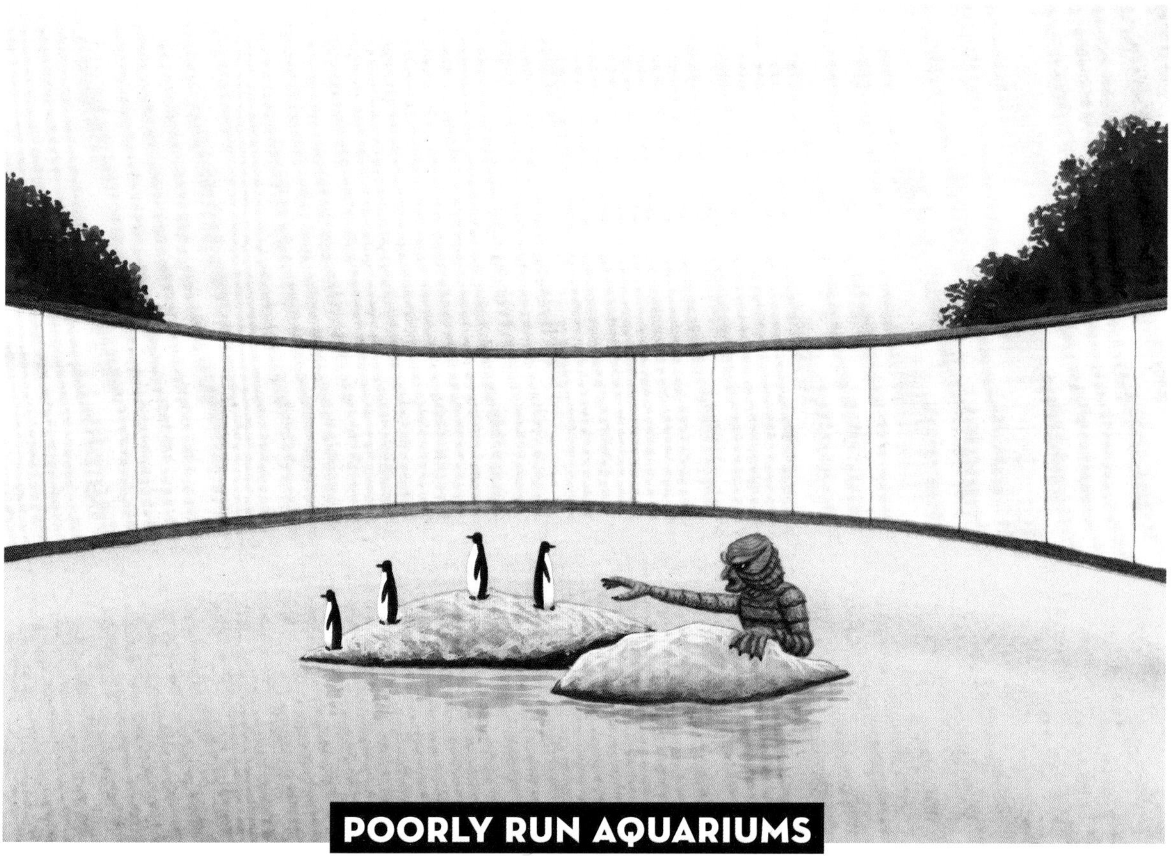

POORLY RUN AQUARIUMS

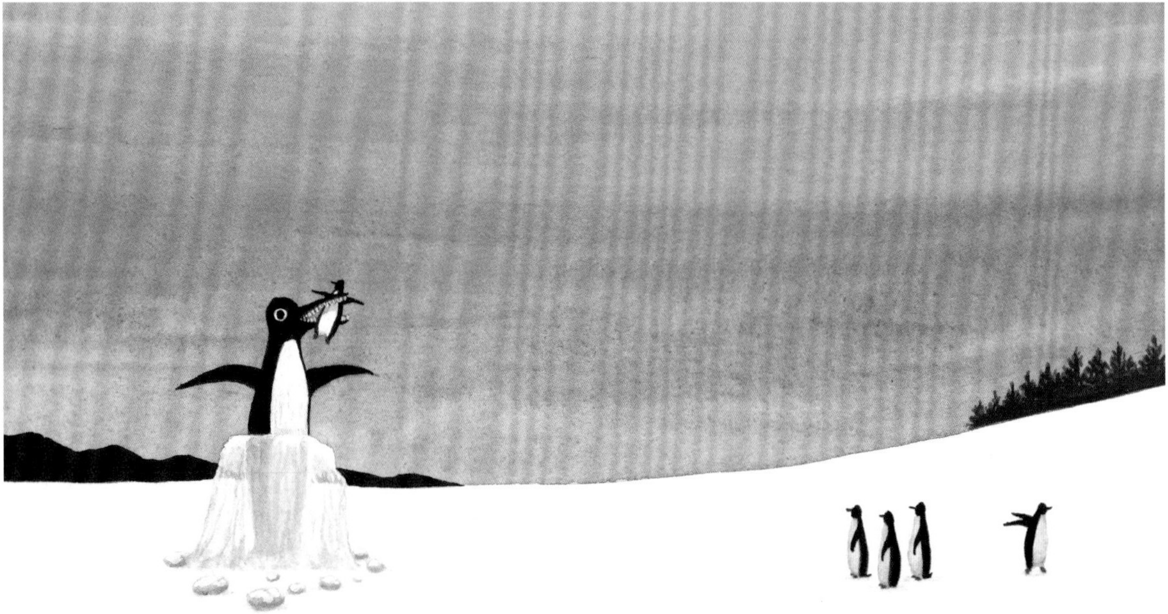

NEWLY DEFROSTED HISTORY

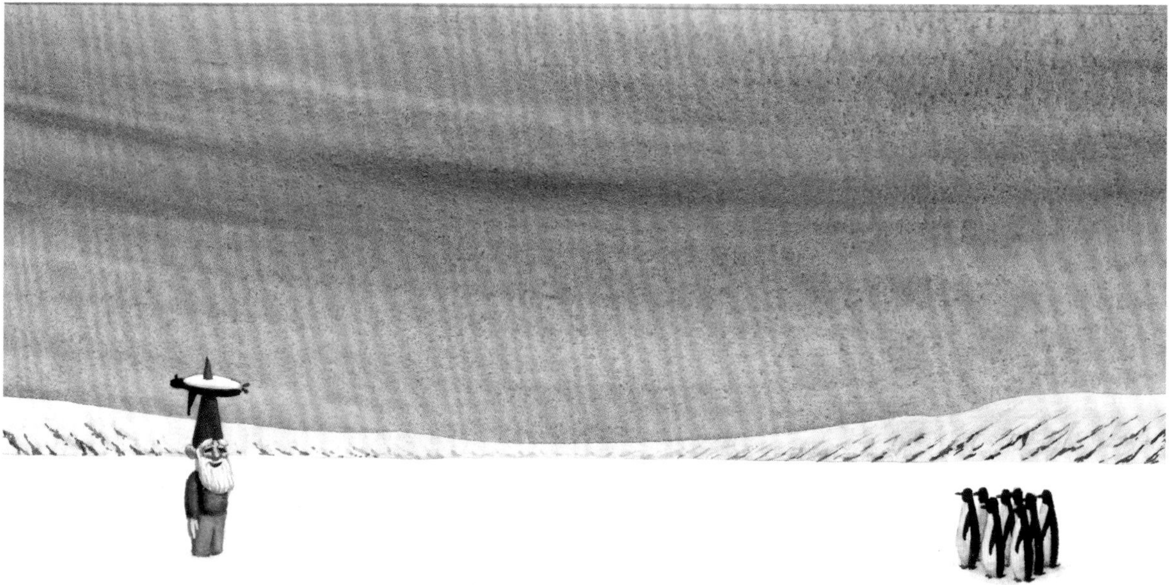

GARDEN GNOMES

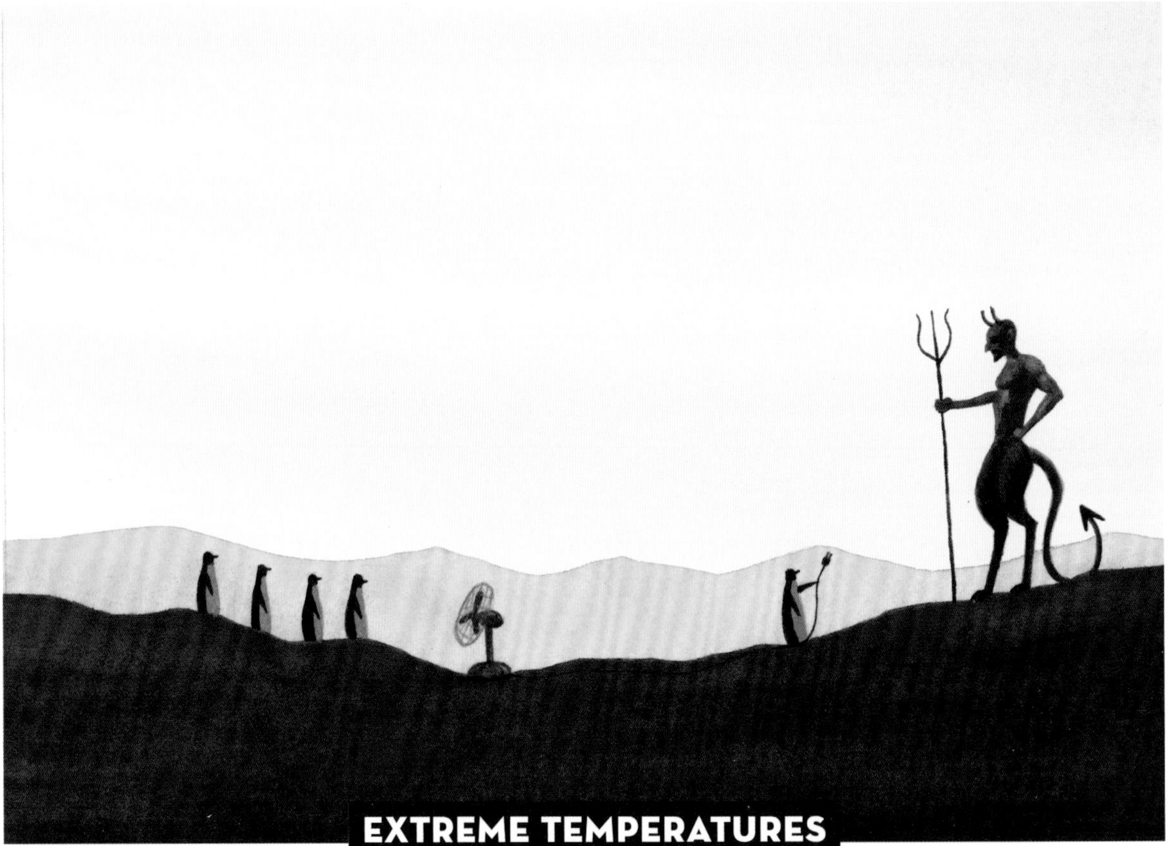

EXTREME TEMPERATURES

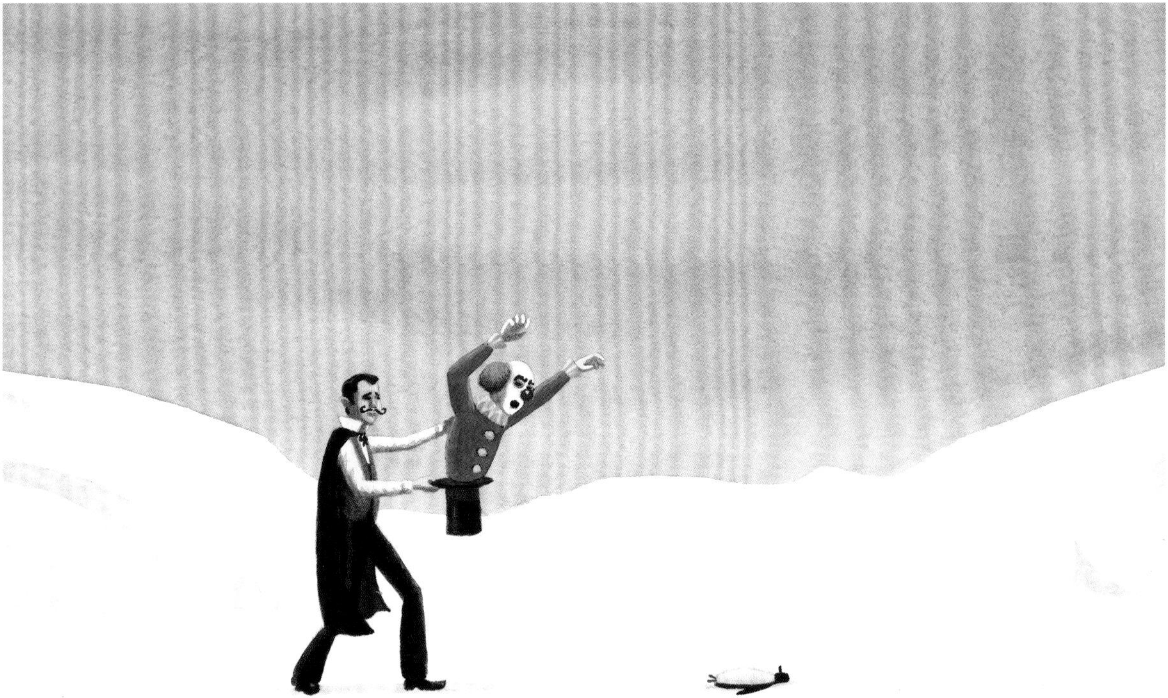

MAGIC TRICKS

PENGUINS
REALLY
REALLY
HATE...

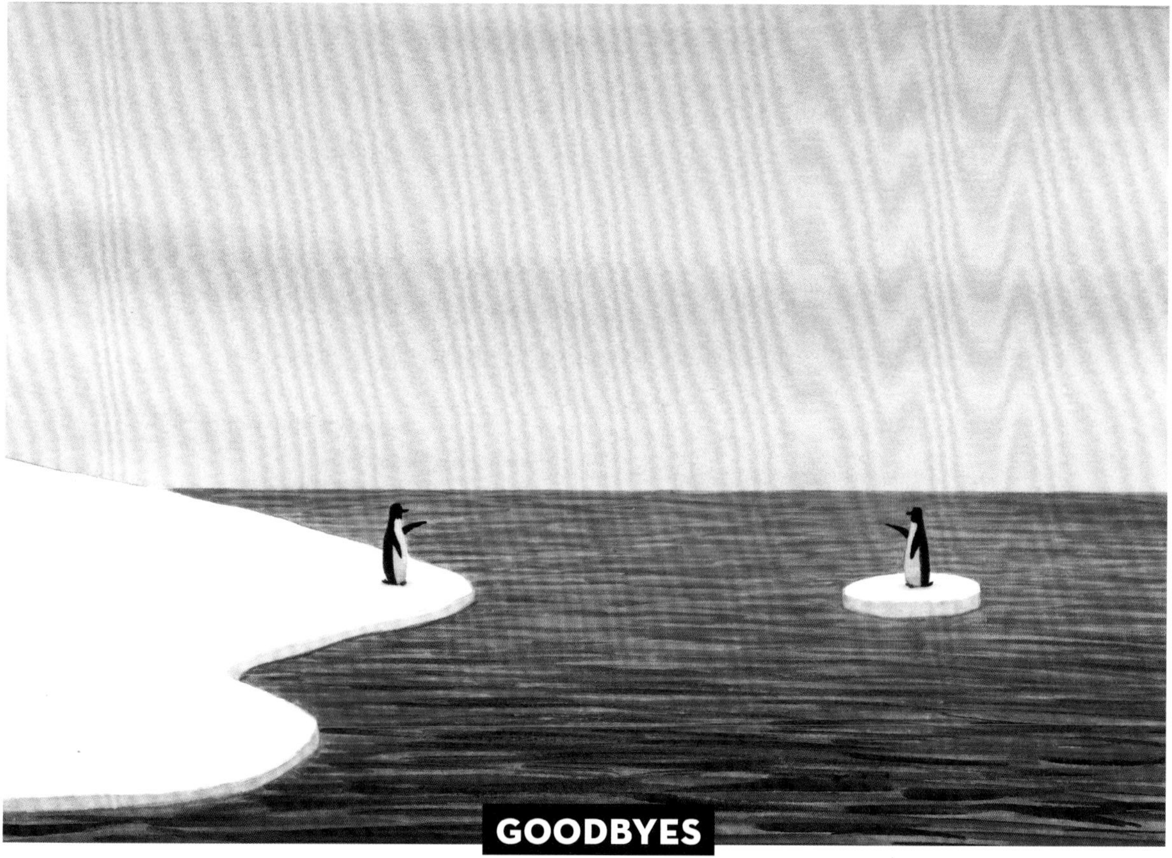

GOODBYES

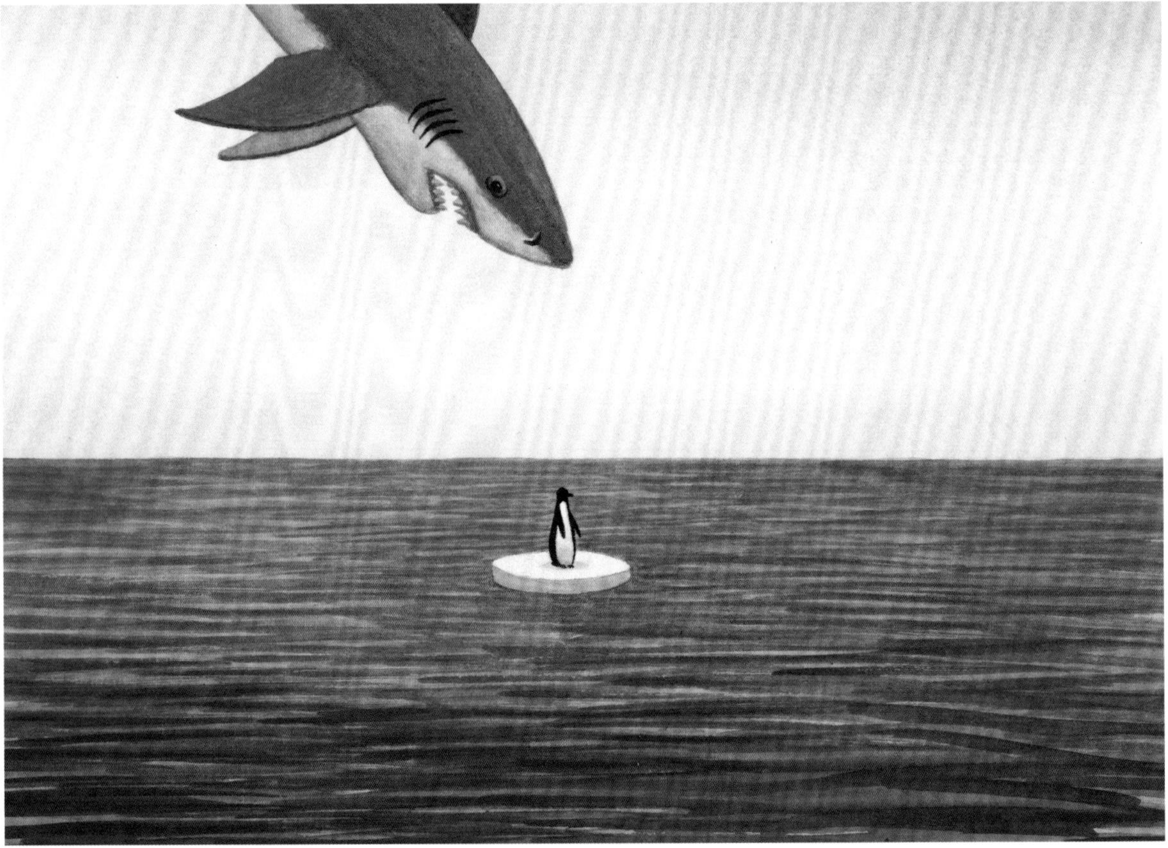